ACKNOWLEDGEMENTS

There are a number of people who have assisted in the preparation of this project to which I am indebted. Specifically, there are several without whose help I could not have completed this work. I wish to thank them for their support.

First I would like to thank my wife Christine for her assistance in editing and typing many of the pages in the final work. Without her time, patience, and support I could not have finished this study.

Next, I would like to express my gratitude to my many Australian friends, some of whom I have never met in person, for their outstanding contributions. Both Tom McIntosh and John Hutton of the Australian Lighthorse Association provided excellent information and assistance over the many miles between here and their country. Their knowledge and expertise saved many additional hours of research. Additionally, the staff of the Australian War Memorial, Canberra, provided kind assistance through correspondence.

Lastly, I would like to thank the staffs of the Combined Arms Research Library at Fort Leavenworth and the Infantry School Library at Fort Benning for their generous assistance locating key texts.

INTRODUCTION

The Australian approach to war has been characterized by initiative and flexibility developed as a result of their unique geographical and cultural background. This study demonstrates the effect of those traits on military tactics and operations.

The development of the Australian traits is contrasted with that of the British with whom they shared a common cultural past. Although the British and Australians have a common cultural tie, the development of the Australians' values was very different. These values caused the Australians to perform differently from tie British under similar circumstances.

During the Boer War and WWI in the Middle East, the Australians and British fought together under the same conditions. The Australians' approach to war proved more successful in both instances and thus set the example for the British. The comparison of the two different military systems during these conflicts makes it easier to show how the Australian traits of initiative and flexibility affected the successful conduct of their operations.

At the turn of the century their organizations and doctrine were virtually the same. In South Africa and particularly in Egypt and Palestine in 1914-1918, the area of

THE AUSTRALIAN LIGHT HORSE

A STUDY OF THE EVOLUTION OF TACTICAL AND OPERATIONAL MANEUVER

by

EDWIN L. KENNEDY, JR., MAJ, USA

U.S. Army Command and General Staff College
Fort Leavenworth, Kansas
1991

The opinions and conclusions expressed herein are those of the author and do not necessarily represent the views of the U.S. Army Command and General Staff College or any other governmental agency.

Table of Contents

Acknowledgements	1
Introduction	2
Chapter 1	5
Chapter 2	65
Chapter 3	119
Chapter 4	149
Chapter 5	175
Equipment List	188
Bibliography	191

operations for the two was identical. This comparison will demonstrate how the Australian mounted infantry was able to successfully adapt to the situation based upon their traits.

Australian initiative and flexibility resulted in tactical innovation which allowed the Australians to change their modus operendii to fit the situation. In a specific battle during the First World War, this occurred even though the Australians used a traditional solution in violation of their own doctrine. The following success had a substantial effect on the outcome of this major battle. More importantly, the tactical success of the Australian mounted troops effected the operational use of all mounted forces in the Eastern Theater for the remainder of WWI. As a result, the complexion of the entire campaign was changed and the role of horse mounted warfare experienced a resurgence after WWI.

The resurgence of the horse mounted forces after the war is unusual within the context of the times. However, the Australians were able to make a serious impact on the conduct of the British cavalry not by changing the British cavalry, but by reinforcing the British cavalry's traditional methods of operation.

The Australians influenced the British cavalry by doing what was thought to be seemingly impossible, that is, to conduct horse mounted charges against a well armed, modern enemy. The success of the Australians affected the British by causing them to reevaluate the role of the horse mounted forces on the modern battlefield. Additionally, it caused the British to disregard their own doctrine for the use of the rifle and revert back to the sword and lance. Interestingly, it also caused the Australians to change their own organizations and weaponry as well.

The transformation of the British cavalry was not lost after the war. A number of other armies used the example of the successes obtained by the British Commonwealth mounted forces in the Middle East to justify the retention of their horse mounted forces.

The Australians never intended to cause such a profound effect on the art of war. In any case, these changes can all be related back to the Australians' approach to war and those traits of initiative and flexibility they used to implement this approach.

CHAPTER 1 - HERITAGE, THE AUSTRALIAN APPROACH TO WAR

Traits of the Australian Soldier

> He is not a soldier as we in London know soldiers. He doesn't like shouldering arms by numbers and votes squad drill 'dam silly.' He is a poor marching man for he has been used to riding. He rides firmly but not gracefully.[1]

To the casual foreign observer in 1914, the Australian military might have been but a clone of the British military. Uniforms, rank, equipment, and arms were virtually identical to the novice observer. Not surprisingly, both British and Australian armies used many of the same manuals, exchanged officers, and Australian officers attended British military schools. Even though both armies appeared similar in most outward manifestations, the Australians developed a military character of their own.[2] This character led to their unique approach to war.

The Australian military tradition developed based upon a number of unique influences. Factors such as culture and geography played major parts in the development of the Australian military heritage. The geography affected the development of the Australians in the areas of health, livelihoods, and the development of cultural traits.[3] Additionally, the pre-federation experiences of the individual Australian states, such as the Boer War, made a major impact upon the Australian military character.

The Australians shared a common cultural heritage with that of the British based upon colonization. However, only a selected and limited portion of the British population initially settled Australia. These were the convicts and middle class free immigrants, which flavored the formation of the Australian culture so differently from that of the British.[4] This happened since the mores and values of the immigrants represented a specific portion of the British population and not a diversified representation. The culture and background of the Australians has therefore had a link to the earliest convict and middle class values. These values eventually permeated all aspects of society and can naturally be found in the Australian military character.

The Australian military character demonstrated in World War One stemmed from the particular background developed by Australians on the island continent during the preceding century. Environmental factors strongly shaped the way the Australians acted and thought, which was different from other peoples, and specifically the people of Britain, where almost all of the early immigrants originated.

Traits which distinguished the Australian soldiers from their British cousins included a natural ability at field craft skills, a collective sense of responsibility, discipline based upon mutual respect, initiative, and flexibility. These traits were noted by both British and Australian military observers and were key to the successes achieved by the Australians during the four years of the campaign in the Eastern Theater. The two most often cited by writers are those of initiative and flexibility.

All of the traits can somehow be linked to the character of the typical Australian. Even though many of the Australians were not from rural areas, the numbers in the mounted infantry (Light Horse) were higher than those in other units due to their familiarity with horses. Even the Australians that were not from rural areas displayed those traits which are attributed to the outback Australians.

While the Australian Light Horsemen were not all from the country, enough were to make a marked difference in their field skill abilities. Turn-of-the-century Australia still exhibited a rural atmosphere. Large areas of unpopulated land separated small towns and cattle or sheep stations in the outback. The development of the Australian continent was not dissimilar to the American West and completely different from that of Britain. The result was that the attitude and skills of the Australian soldiers reflected rural and pioneer values.[5]

Britain was a small island, considerably more crowded than Australia, and contained a number of large urban areas. There were few parts of Britain that were unsettled. Unlike Britons, a large number of Australians were involved in work in the sparsely settled areas and became accustomed to working the land outdoors. Used to traveling long distances between populated locales, and working the outback, many Australians developed skills associated with rural life such as riding, dead reckoning navigation, and basic survival. It was a compilation of these experiences that gave the Australian soldiers their skills such as land navigation cited by commanders in the war.[6]

Cultural heritage also played a factor in the development of the Australian which was different from that of the British. Begun as a colonial settlement by the British in 1788 for their convict population, it reflected many of the values of the convict derivative population in terms of its socialization. A "collectivist" tendency developed among those people sent to settle Australia in which they pitted themselves against the bureaucrats and soldiers sent to administer them.[7] This "collectivist" tendency caused differences in the development of the Australian society from that of the British.

The social background of the convict population tended to force a class system to develop much differently than in the other colonies established by the British. The background of the convicts was largely urban in nature. Additionally, those reported to Australia generally came from the same bottom portion of the society in Britain. This common background and experience caused a bonding of the peoples (collective socialism) instead of a stratification based upon wealth, privilege, or station.

The upper class of people in Australia developed from the government administrators and colonial entrepeneurs. A number of free colonists established herds of sheep and cattle at stations. Known as "squatters", they became part of the new upper class due to their relative wealth. The squatters provided jobs for numbers of people to include freed convicts as station hands and shearers.

Their common class background established a group of peoples who were able to begin anew without the social strata of their home country. While a class system did evolve, it certainly was not as stifling nor as rigid as that they had experienced in Britain. The new "upper class" were the middle class merchants, land owners, and administrators. These free men were intent upon maintaining their respectable status and therefore did little mingling with the convict population.[8]

The squatters provided work for large numbers of itinerant workers known as "swagmen." These workers looked for seasonal employment on the stations shearing sheep or working cattle. Because there were no labor organizations to handle disputes or issues, the swagmen developed informal groups to represent themselves against the depredations (perceived and real) of the upper class squatters. A feeling of collective responsibility for the group with a common interest developed in this way.

Uniquely Australian, and tied to this phenomena, was the tradition of "mateship." "Mateship" describes the close affinity that a small group of men had for each other due to their common situation. Normally two, but sometimes more, men were "mates" and developed a pair-bonding said to have initiated during the time convicts were kept together in pairs in order to help each other out. The concept depended upon the reliance of those who were "mates" to support the other and recognized the inability of individuals to survive by themselves in the earliest days of the colony.[9] This particular trait became ingrained in the Australian culture and survives to this day.

While the Australians developed traits such as the collectivism which might seem to contradict independence, they in fact developed an intense independence as a trait. Having been the subjects of a severe legal system which granted few individual rights, the colonial Australians were quick to develop a feeling of individualism and resented any violation of their personal freedoms.[10] Additionally, they were cast into a frontier situation as early settlers and quickly had to adapt to harsh conditions in order to survive.

Forced to fend for themselves in an undeveloped land, the early colonists learned that they were responsible for their own survival. No established markets, produce, or services existed. The tremendous distance to England precluded the support required of people taken from a fully developed country and thrust into a completely undeveloped land. In order to survive, people had to quickly adapt and develop skills required to exist. Those who failed to participate perished. Those who immigrated as free men had only to take advantage of the opportunities a new country offered and those who had no drive would have been unable to succeed. Large areas of land were available for the taking and the free colonists that desired to work hard could make a place for himself. Initiative, therefore, became a trait of necessity.[11]

An Australian military trait which was most commonly mentioned in writings of the war periods had to do with their form of discipline (or lack thereof depending upon the perspective). In most British writings, this trait is strongly criticized.[12] Among Australian writers, it is generally acknowledged as a strength of the Australian character.

Although the British view of Australian discipline has historically been uncomplimentary, it was based upon a perspective which was very different from that of the Australians. In the Australians' background, men were accepted for their deeds, and, allegiance was gained by reputation and acts, not titles, money, or education. This was very different from that of the turn of the century British system.[13] Although the purchase of commissions in the British Army had been done away with, there were vestiges of the gentleman's caste in which connections and money still played a part of being an officer. Individual officers might display those attributes considered necessary for leaders today; however, the overall feeling was that soldiering for officers was still a gentlemen's endeavor and the bond between the officer and his soldiers was not as keen as it was in the Australian system.

Australian soldiers placed a much greater value on solutions to problems that made practical sense. Educated leaders meant little if they could not apply their common sense to solve problems. Australian leaders were expected to use common sense and if they did not, they lost their effectiveness.

Discipline of soldiers was engendered by good leadership and not the King's regulations or threat of punishment. Additionally, the Australians had an established tradition by the mid-nineteenth century of popular leadership and volunteer military service in the militia units.

Until small regular army units were formed, military

service was in militia or volunteer units. In the militia, leaders were selected by the members of the unit. Leaders tended to be selected on their savvy and not their educational or family backgrounds. This was completely antithetical to British regular forces where leaders were selected by higher authority and designated, not voted into position. Discipline was achieved by the leaders in the Australian militia units being able to demonstrate competence and ability to the members of the unit. Bad leaders did not last long and discipline was based upon mutual respect.[14]

Discipline in the Australian Army was not manifested by factors such as the appearance of the soldier on the drill square. Instead, it was demonstrated by the ability of the soldiers to willingly perform their actions without orders or direction. The Australian soldier was loath to follow orders which made no apparent sense or a leader who would not listen to his subordinates. This intolerance of ineptitude would become a collective hallmark of Australian soldiers.

Contrast the Australian system with the military system of the nineteenth and early twentieth century British Army and their method of exacting discipline. The British system depended primarily upon the legal status of the leader, not necessarily demonstrated competence.[15]

While the British commissioning system allowed for

those who were educated or technically competent to become leaders by virtue of rank or title, it generally provided few mechanisms to insure that those who were not good leaders from securing commissions. The result was that until WWI the British Army depended upon draconian regulations and the power of deterrence for discipline when the leadership fell short. Attempted reforms from within the army did little to change this system. There existed a discernable difference between the British and Australian systems at the beginning of WWI for these reasons. Both were successful in their own contexts.

An innate ability at field craft, a collective sense of responsibility for the group, initiative and flexibility born of necessity in a tough environment, and a form of discipline which today seems very common sense but was a radical departure from traditional British norms, all combined to make up the character of the Australian military man. These traits are some of the ones more commonly cited. While not all inclusive, they highlight some of the more obvious traits. Of these, the ones that had the greatest impact on military operations were those of initiative and flexibility.

The Australian and His Horse

> On arriving in England he was sent to a riding school for one week. When the horses were

issued, it was found that only one Australian had not been on a horse before (out of forty).[16]

To the Australian the horse was not only a means of transportation but a means of livelihood. Settlements and cattle stations were separated by long distances. Horses became the primary means of transportation for thousands of Australians who learned how to ride at a very young age. In the "outback," where the ranching industry had established itself, the graziers (cattle raisers) completely depended upon the horse for its utility.

Unlike today, when the horse is very seldom used for anything but sport and pleasure, it provided the means of livelihood for herders and transportation for thousands in nineteenth and early twentieth century Australia. From a modest beginning of seven horses in 1788, the horse population had increased by the end of the Boer War to 450,125.[17] The utility of the horse was tremendous in a country of three million square miles and a population density of about one person per square mile.

The horse of choice for the Australians was the native bred "Waler." Named after the state in which the horse was originally raised (New South Wales). A cross between several breeds but with a strong thoroughbred bloodline, the horse produced consisted of the best characteristics of the different breeds raised in Australia. Unlike the British cavalry horses, the Waler was raised on grass pasture alone. The British cavalry horses, though of good lineage, were stalled and developed those problems associated with horses not able to roam free. The Waler became inured to the outdoors and a diet of grass whereas the British cavalry horses became dependent upon grain feeds and hay.[18]

The difference the methods of raising the horses brought about were not obvious until the horses were tested on campaign. Those horses that were treated with what would seem like more apparent care, the British cavalry mounts, were the ones more apt to fail under the rigors of field conditions. The Walers, used to being kept outdoors and free to exercise, were found to be more resilient and recovered from hard work more quickly.[19]

The Australian Walers were bred in an environment which was similar to the environments they would serve in during both the Boer and the First World Wars. The Walers' acclimatization to dry grasslands in the outback of Australian certainly prepared them better for the campaign rigors than the horses of the British cavalry which had been stabled raised and watered in a moderate European climate.

The horse became a part of the Australian military as a necessity. The Australians formed mounted units to solve the defense problem of moving long distances in an undeveloped country with limited transportation networks.[20] Instead of horse cavalry, they opted for mounted infantry, or Light Horse. A fairly large number of units were formed, no doubt, based upon the familiarity of the volunteers with horses.

Mounted infantry had been developed as early as the American Civil War. Units that were specifically trained as infantry were given preemptory riding instruction and formed into "mounted infantry." The British adopted the system sometime in the 1870s and it quickly caught on in Australia.

The difference between mounted infantry and cavalry was fairly substantial initially. Mounted infantry were an <u>ad hoc</u> organization given horses, mules, or, in some cases, camels, to improve their mobility. The means of transportation, whatever animal was used, was only designed to facilitate the infantryman's ability to move to the battlefield. The infantryman dismounted and fought as he normally would once he arrived at the battle site.

Cavalrymen were trained to ride to the battle and then fight mounted from their horses if necessary. The cavalry was expected to perform a number of tasks from their horses only dismounting to fight under unusual circumstances. The primary mission of the cavalry was to provide shock action by closing with the enemy mounted. They performed additional tasks such as reconnaissance and security missions which was complemented by their mobility and speed.

Cavalrymen were armed differently from mounted infantry as a result of their difference in missions. Cavalry were equipped with swords or sabers, pistols, lances, and carbines. Mounted infantry was equipped with the rifle and bayonet. Hence the basic difference was not only in their doctrinal employment, but in their armament as well. Only at the end of the nineteenth century would the tactical employment of the cavalry begin to change to more of a dismounted role. In most armies their armament did not match the change in tactics and the limited range carbine was retained until after the turn of the century.

In the early twentieth century, the skill of riding was still transferable to the military and a number of men enlisted in Light Horse units for that reason. This is to be contrasted to the British Army whereby soldiers had to be trained how to ride due to the relative unfamiliarity with the horse. This skill played an important part of the Australians' role later during the Boer War when horse mobility became a major factor.

The Formation of the Australian Army

> The serving soldiers . . . especially in the Australian colonies . . . were often called upon to perform police duties, which did not endear them to the public . . . .[21]

The background of the convicts who had been forcibly relocated to Australia by transporting (removal from Britain by force) led to a common low regard for those who were superior in social status and who were in positions of authority. The rough treatment of the convicts by the military and employers (the administrators and small entrepeneurs) in Australia, induced a strong dislike for both the military and authority.[22]

The dislike for soldiers and policemen was a natural reaction to the abuses of power that these elements inflicted on the first settlers.[23] The enforcers of European civil law at the turn of the eighteenth century, when Australia was founded as a penal colony, were the military. The soldiers were the enforcement arm of the judicial system in Britain and accompanied the first colonists to Australia. During the ninety years of its presence in Australia, the British Army was used to subdue civil disturbances and enforce jurisprudence. It is no wonder then, that the feelings of the Australian settlers were generally anti-military during the early days of settlement.

Since the British Army garrisons remained relatively small for the size of the area to be administered in Australia, the free population of the separate Australian states began to explore ways to protect themselves. When no serious external threats existed, the Australians were certainly happy enough to allow the British government to shoulder the burden for overall defense.[24] During the mid and late nineteenth century, however, foreign exploration in the South Pacific led to concerns of possible conflict.[25] This aroused the concern of the immigrants who may have lacked confidence in the British navy to protect their interests.

By the mid-nineteenth century the use of Australia as a penal colony ceased and a large number of free immigrants began to arrive. The number of non-convict settlers (to include convict progeny) began to gradually outnumber those that were convicts.[26] Britain began to expect the Australian states (as a single country did not exist as yet) to share a greater proportion of the defense costs including the provisioning of troops.

The response was the formation of non-regular state units. The first organized citizen military units had been formed in 1840 but existed haphazardly as the need arose. In addition to avoiding the formation of a professional standing military, the separate Australian states could save money by forming part time citizen military forces as they did. The traditional English fear of a standing army had no doubt been transplanted by the British colonists, both free and convict.[27] This fear was felt even more strongly by the convicts who had been particularly abused by the soldiers in the early garrisons. The separate states were also able to save a substantial amount of money by not forming a professional military. Full time forces would require full time pay and benefits. There were other options that could prove to be more economically feasible and still provide a military force.

The answer to the formation of a military establishment for defense was solved by two different methods. Militia units were formed and manned by a ballot system. The militia cost the individual Australian states only the equipment and salary for those called to duty. Another solution was the system of "volunteer units" which proved more popular than the militia. Volunteers, as the name implies, were not selected by ballot, and therefore were truly participatory of their own free will unlike the militia. Volunteers provided their own arms, ammunition, and equipment.[28] Because participation was strictly up to the individual, it better suited the Australians than the mandated system of the militia.

In 1870 Britain removed all of its forces from the Australian colonies.[29] This forced the states to consider supplementing the existing systems of militia and volunteer units providing for the states' defense. German claims in adjoining islands and exploration by other European powers raised concerns as to the vulnerability of the colonies to exploitation by foreign military powers. The perceived threat from imperialistic European powers with designs on unclaimed areas of the Pacific region caused the Australians to consider increasing the number and type of citizen forces which had only been loosely formed prior to 1870.

The removal of the British forces caused a number of problems for the Australians. While the people lived in the same country, it was not yet a nation but a group of colonial states joined by geographic boundaries. Each state had its own separate government, finances, rail, and military systems. Because there was no single national authority, cooperation between states occurred based upon perceived common problems and good will.

Each state formed its own military units according to its own needs and ability to finance them. Serious consideration for the establishment of standing state military forces did not really begin until 1870 with the departure of the British Army. As can be imagined, proposals for the composition and missions of the military forces were the objects of intense debates. The inherited distrust of the standing military and the power it represented were well ingrained in the average Australian.

The costs of maintaining regular forces proved to be a constant drain on the states' finances. The militia or volunteer systems, which required an initial outlay and then a smaller amount to maintain it, was popular with the states. The states eventually formed very small regular forces under the auspices of the individual state governments.

Individual states were responsible for their own administration because Australia was not yet a nation with a centralized government. Defense matters were naturally handled by the states. Victoria and New South Wales raised the first regular forces after the departure of the British Army. Maintenance costs associated with the standing forces caused the formation and disbandment of the regular forces within a short time. A mild recession at the end of the nineteenth century forced major cutbacks in the funding of the regular forces and several were eliminated or reduced in size.[30] Only small artillery units (batteries) were kept for coastal defense as part of the regular military. These units were paid to remain on full time duty, were uniformed, fed and armed by the states to which they belonged. Unlike the militia and volunteer units, their officers were schooled in a manner similar to those of the British regular army.[31]

In 1885 the war in the Sudan between Britain and the forces of the Mahdi erupted when the city of Khartoum was besieged. The British sent a relief expedition under General Kitchener but it arrived too late to prevent the fall of the city. New South Wales responded to the war by sending a reinforced infantry battalion and two batteries of artillery on short notice.

Significantly, this constituted the first major overseas deployment of Australians on a military expedition. While the Australians arrived too late to take part in any serious fighting, their willingness to participate set a precedence for future wars.[32]

The majority of military force available to the state governments remained the militia and volunteer units. Professional British Army officers were assigned to Australia to assist in the formation of military units, training, and to remain in command overall. The Australian state governments realized the need for coordination in defense matters based upon the geographic proximity to one another. They resolved the problem of decentralized military effort by formally coordinating the employment of their forces in case of war. This was accomplished by joint state conferences where agreements were made regarding the command, control, and deployment of each states' forces in case of conflict.[33]

Further standardization between state forces was attempted after 1889. A mandated inspection visit by a regular British officer, Major-General Brian Edwards, resulted in a consolidated recommendation for improvement of state forces. His recommendations for standardized brigade formations across state boundaries as well as a plan to mobilize forces by rail furthered the effort to centralize military union of the separate state forces.[34]

Military development continued over the next few years and the states began to take on the challenge of forming their own military forces. By the end of the nineteenth century the foundations of the modern Australian military were being laid. Already, the establishment of citizen forces in lieu of standing regular formations was the norm. An officer education system was established in each state and officers were trained by British officers or in British or Indian Army military schools.

The citizen army organizations of the militia or volunteers suited the Australians who were rather proud of their freedoms. Lacking the formality and bureaucracy of standing armies, leadership by popular vote (in volunteer units), and looser discipline fitting the nature of the independent minded Australians, all combined to influence the Australian military formations of the post-1870 era.

What evolved from the first experiences of the Australian Army were popular state armies with a character different from that of the British who had played, and still strongly influenced, the formation of the state military forces. The character of these forces were influenced by the factors which made the people different from the British. Although they shared a common cultural heritage of language, law, customs, and economic systems, their geographic and new cultural environment combined to create uniquely Australian military traditions.

First, there was the tradition of voluntary military participation exemplified by the volunteer and militia units. Eventually the two systems melded and units took on the characteristics of the volunteer units in regards to voluntary participation. Voluntary participation in the military would be a cornerstone of the Australian military system for years to come, even during the height of the two world wars.[35]

Secondly, the matter of discipline was not just a trait of individual Australian soldiers, but a institutionalized characteristic of the Australian units. Discipline revolved around two distinct factors, "mateship" and trust in the leadership. Australians viewed discipline much more pragmatically than the British in that the real test was on the battlefield, not the drill square. Appearance and the outward manifestations of servitude (such as saluting) did not equate to the Australians view of discipline. What counted to the Australians was the conduct of the soldier under fire. They all shared the belief that competent leadership begat loyalty and discipline and that there was a very low tolerance for incompetence among leaders.[36]

The military tradition of volunteer forces became the hallmark of the Australian system. The resulting issue of the

Australian form of discipline would become a point of contention numerous times during the Boer and First World Wars between the British and Australians. Australians would eventually overcome the problem in their own way and British commanders would learn to live with it.

The Boer War and Australia

The Imperial officers did not know their quality. They speedily found, however, that as mounted infantry and for scouting work the Australian has no superiors.[37]

When the Australian states approached the twentieth century, they did so with their own individual states' military systems. Although not politically united, they were united in other manners such as language and culture. Australia entered the Boer War in 1899 as separate colonial states and emerged as a unified nation in 1902.

By the end of the nineteenth century the separate colonial states of Australia were cooperating on matter such as defense. A move to unite the separate Australian states into one nation under the title of "federation" gained momentum as the problems for the British in South Africa culminated in the final war of a series with the Boers, 1899-1902. The importance of this war with regards to both the British and the Australians is that it set the stage for their entry into World War I.

The initial British approach to the war in South Africa

suffered many deficiencies which were the results of poor planning and inflexibility. The British entered the last war with Boers in 1899 with the lessons learned from the previous conflicts, the last fought eighteen years earlier. Significant strides in military technology had occurred since that time which were not considered by the British.

As an example of the effect of technology on the Anglo-Boer conflicts, the armies fielded by the British in the previous Boer conflicts had won by employing massed infantry, artillery and a small amount of cavalry.[38] The Boers had lost the earlier conflicts more as a result of their own faults than the military prowess of the British. The fact remains that the Boers failed and the British succeeded. The British took away the wrong lessons from their successes.

An analysis of how the British succeeded against the Boers might partially explain why the same techniques and tactics were tried again in 1899 in South Africa. In a fairly large engagement which occurred in 1848, a British Army unit composed of infantry, mounted rifles (colonial mounted infantry), and artillery, decisively beat a force which was at least equal in size if not larger than the 600 man British force.[39]

Technology had a great deal to do with the defeat of the Boers by the British who used massed infantry to close on the Boer positions. In 1848, the smoothbore musket was still the primary shoulder weapon in use throughout the world. The Boers, who purchased their own weapons individually, probably had either percussion rifles or muskets. The British were still using muskets as they had been for a number of years in standard line units. Both the rifles and muskets of the time took an exceedingly long time to reload and fire. The musket had a poor reputation for accuracy accounting for the short engagement distances of 100 meters or less. While the rifle's accuracy was greater, the trade-off was the time necessary to reload which was greater than that of the musket's.

Combined with the short engagement range to the British and the fact that the British would close with the bayonet after firing a volley, the Boers would have been hard pressed to withstand a massed infantry assault unless they outnumbered the British substantially more than they did in this situation or were able to slow or stop the British assault. Since precise details of the existing accounts are not readily available, some assumptions can be made as to how the Boers were defeated.

The British accounts show that the Boers dismounted from their horses. The Boer plan had been to ambush the British at short distance around a road leading into a creek.

Assuming that the Boers fired on the British at about 100 meters it would have taken at least 20 seconds for a well trained man to reload the musket and fire again. In those twenty seconds the British theoretically could have fired a volley and then closed with the bayonet if intervening terrain did not hinder a dismounted charge.

What actually happened is that Boers were over-run before they could reach their horses located to the rear of their positions. They probably attempted to reload to fire again but the British infantry was upon them before they could get away.[40]

The lessons of this engagement stuck with the British for a number of years. They failed to consider the change that the breech loading or magazine fed rifle would bring to the battlefield. The battles of the next war with the Boers in 1881 should have alerted the British that the factors which had made them successful in 1848 were no longer valid. Several severe defeats culminating in a political settlement did not change the British Army's methods, and they left the second campaign in 1881 thinking that the methods of massed infantry were still valid.(41)

Salient to their defeats in 1881 was the change in weaponry used by the Boers. While the Boers were armed with a number of different rifles, the photographs of the types they had show that they were of the most modern variety of breechloaders. [42] The extended range of modern rifles out to about one thousand meters made a marked difference in the tactics used by the Boers. Greater engagement ranges combined with a higher rate of fire meant that the British infantry formations would have to cover ten times the distance under fire then when they fought the Boers in 1848. This advance would have to occur under a barrage of fire from a rate which increased from three rounds per minute to about six to ten aimed rounds per minute. Additionally, the Boers could fight more dispersed and use the ground as cover as it would not be necessary to stand and reload as it was in 1848.

The setbacks suffered by the British in 1881 were repeated in some of the same places almost twenty years later against the same foes. The widespread use of the magazine fed rifle in the intervening years, coupled with the mobility of the Boer, was never planned for by the conservative British officer corps. While the British Army continued to plan for a war against poorly trained and equipped tribesmen and conventional European enemies (although their methods for doing so were questionable), the Boers developed a new style of warfare for which the British were wholly unprepared.[43]

The war resulted in doctrinal and equipment changes to the British Army. To the Australians, the Boer War served to validate their tactics, methods, and organizations. After the war, the British made changes to organizations, tactics, equipment, and uniforms in response to their lessons learned in South Africa.⁴⁴ The Australians did not have to make many changes at all. The effects of the Boer War set the stage for the entry of both the British and Australians into the First World War and is important for this reason.

For the British and Australians, South Africa was the last major military action prior to the First World War. Several senior British and Australian commanders were to receive valuable experience on the veldts of South Africa. This experience would later stand them in good stead in the Middle East but would be wholly inappropriate for use in Europe.⁴⁵ While the British commanders may have learned a great deal in South Africa, they may have learned the wrong lessons for a war in Europe.

The British Army discovered that mobility was the key to the success in South Africa. Equipping infantry with horses provided a greater relative mobility than foot mobile troops. Their mobility at least matched that of the elusive Boers. Not only was mobility key and essential, but the means to achieve it, the horse, became key and essential also.

The renewal of horse cavalry's importance was predicated on the fact that it was specifically trained to conduct mounted warfare as it was conducted in the latter stages of the war in South Africa. By the end of the Boer War it was being used as a shock, exploitation, and pursuit force.

Mobility was one of the keys to success in South Africa. The cavalry and the mounted infantry happened to use the horse as a means of mobility. Mounted infantry eventually became more prevalent than cavalry during the war. The difference was lost on the British commanders who equated the success gained by horse mounted units to the cavalry, not the mounted infantry.

The deductions of the British commanders were that mobility led to success (a fairly accurate assessment). The horse was responsible for the relative mobility (correct again), the cavalry was the primary horse mounted branch (senior but not as numerous); therefore, the cavalry was obviously the root cause of the success. But these were the wrong lessons. The British overwhelmed the Boers with mounted units, cavalry and mounted infantry.

The minor tactical successes of the cavalry were due more to the conditions of the beaten and retreating Boers than to the proper environment for cavalry. British mounted infantry flourished in South Africa but disappeared from the British Army soon after the Boer War as the cavalry proponents gained influence. Mounted infantry disappeared from the British Army but remained the backbone of the Australian forces just as they had been prior to the war.

Perhaps part of the problem of the British commanders was their failure to connect the fact that all horse mounted forces (mounted infantry specifically) did not necessarily mean cavalry and success of mounted forces was not necessarily the success of "cavalry." The success of the British forces in South Africa had, in great part, been accomplished by mounted infantry, not cavalry.

Unfortunately, the British commanders made an illogical deduction from the generalized success of horse mounted forces and assumed that the overall success gained by horse mounted forces applied to the small number of cavalry units as well. In this regard, they then rationalized the maintenance of cavalry forces after the war, but not mounted infantry.

In the year prior to the 1899-1902 Boer War, the British again conducted a major campaign in the Sudan. Massed infantry tactics (the square) and the cavalry armed with edged weapons decided the campaign at Omdurman in 1898 much as it had done at Waterloo.

However, fighting Dervishes was different than fighting the Boers. The Dervishes fought en masse against weapons such as Gatling guns, artillery, and well trained infantry that would stand its ground. Preferring to close with the British in hand-to-hand combat, the Dervishes were the perfect target for the British soldiers and their massive firepower.

The Boers were better armed and used the terrain to their advantage to prevent being engaged by the massed infantry firing in volleys. Additionally, the horse mounted Boers used their relatively superior mobility against British infantry. They could ride away before they could be engaged in close combat, thus maintaining their freedom of maneuver.

The style of warfare used by the Boers was greatly affected by their cultural patterns and the geography of their land. In fact, the geographic factors affected the Boers in a fashion similar to the way it affected the Australians. Largely a farming class people, the Boers' familiarity with the outdoors was a definite advantage to their struggle. The area of South Africa where they settled was largely grassland with sparse vegetation. In the South African veldt the rolling grasslands and open terrain offered long range observation, fields of fire, and excellent mobility to mounted forces.

The rural background of the Boers created a situation where dependence upon firearms and the horse became absolute requirements. Firearms were important because of the constant danger of fighting with the native tribes and horses because of the great distances between settlements and towns on the veldt. The Boers as a whole were accomplished horsemen and were all mounted with the exception of those in the artillery and trains.

In order to protect themselves prior to the conflict with the British, the Boers formed themselves into irregular groups of men under elected leaders. Armed with modern magazine weapons from countries such as Germany, the Boers became the nemesis of the British forces. Boer horse mounted mobility and tactics made the superior discipline and relative firepower of the opposing British Army less effective in the initial stages of the war.[46]

The Boers fought a series of engagements and battles in which the British had difficulty in trying to close by using massed formations. Even the British cavalry units were at a disadvantage since they could rarely find a body of Boers to charge. The Boer rifles outranged the British cavalry carbines by several hundred yards which placed the British at a definite disadvantage when fighting dismounted. The Boers used the stand-off range of modern, high velocity rifles and fought only when the terms suited them. Mounting and riding away when the British infantry approached, the Boers managed to generally avoid decisive combat in which the British could muster the advantage of massed firepower.[47]

A change to the tactics and techniques used by the British solved the disparity caused by the new method of warfare. It took time but the British began to realize after the first six months that bringing the Boers to bay and defeating them with conventional infantry tactics was not the best solution. The problem not only lay in the rigid tactics the British used but their lack of relative mobility.

The British gradually changed their tactics and the mobility problem was addressed by the mounting of large numbers of infantry on horses. The British hoped that they could at least match the mobility of the Boers with mounted infantry. The problem was not so easily solved however. Placing a soldier on a horse is only one small part of making him a useful and efficient mounted soldier. Mounted infantry had been used previously but it had taken time and training to convert them.[48] The British faced the same problems again. It was this very problem that the Australians solved.

The British Minister for War Lord Lansdowne sent the first request for assistance to the Australians in 1899. Critically underestimating both the nature of the war and the ability of the Australians, he requested that primarily infantry be sent.[49] Initial requests to the Australian states for assistance were quickly honored. Again, as in 1885, the state of New South Wales made the first contribution when its lancer regiment was sent to South Africa directly from training at Aldershot in England.[50]

The Australians adapted to their new settings well since

South Africa was similar to portions of Australia in many respects. Both had large areas of sparsely populated land. The area of South Africa in which the war was fought stood on the same latitude as the central part of the most populated portions of eastern Australia, thereby giving it many of the same characteristics. The weather and terrain were probably reminiscent of the grasslands of Queensland and New South Wales to many Australians.[51]

Like their Boer adversaries, the Australians were outdoorsmen and many Australians were as at home on the veldt as they were in the outback. So successful were the initial contingents of Australian horse mounted soldiers that the British rescinded the priority of requested troops and asked for all mounted troops instead. Fighting in numerous small skirmishes, the Australians were able to establish a reputation for fighting the Boers on their own terms. Using the horse for tactical mobility, the Australian soldiers dismounted, sniped, ambushed and fought the Boers in open order, not massed formations.[52]

The reason the British requested more Australians, in lieu of mounting additional infantry of their own, becomes more obvious when considering the massive number of British horse casualties. Many of the horses were lamed by extremely poor management and horsemanship. In the exigency of South

Africa, the British infantryman did not have time to be formally trained to care for his horse to the standards of the cavalry. Large numbers of horses fell victim to sore backs and other related disabling ailments caused by inexperience.[53]

Sore backs can be caused by more than poor management (grooming and feeding) and the comments from the war regarding the poor horsemanship of the British mounted infantry was a detriment to the health of the horses as well as the conduct of the operations. Unable to train properly in the art of horsemanship, the mounted infantry had its work cut out just trying to stay on the horses. Moving at a trot cross country would have been difficult at best for untrained mounted infantry.[54]

The fastest sustained march pace that could be obtained from such troops was an extended walk, about four miles per hour. This is faster than normal infantry but not by much. Additionally, the mounted infantry used an awkward rifle bucket, subsequently discarded after the war because of its lack of utility. Carrying the rifle in this appurtenance required the right arm to balance the rifle by the sling in its bucket located on the off-side of the saddle. This arrangement was unsatisfactory since the right arm could not then grasp the reins correctly without pulling the rifle barrel forward.

If the mounted infantryman was not issued a rifle

bucket, as some photographs indicate, then the rifles were slung over the shoulder, or carried on the pommel of the saddle. Carrying a rifle with one hand would leave only one to manage the reins of the horse. This predicament would certainly not have availed itself to a non-horseman.

The large complement of Australians already trained to ride was obviously a benefit to the prevention of rider induced lameness on horses. The type of riding demonstrated by the Australians might not have compared favorably to the well drilled British cavalry units but it was effective. British cavalrymen spent hours drilling in equitation and formation riding. Cavalry tactics demanded that horsemen maintain close interval for the ultimate clash, the charge. British cavalry was trained to ride boot-to-boot in order to optimize the mass of the horse during a charge. Additionally, formations looked military, a factor that cannot be overlooked in the nineteenth century British Army.

The Australians were "natural" riders who had learned their skill through necessity at home. A large number of Australians depended upon the horse for transportation and knew how to ride as a normal skill. For these reasons the finer points of riding were overlooked as the purpose of the horse was strictly for transportation to the battlefield. For example, pictures of the Australians show them typically slouching in their saddles with their legs extended forward in a comfortable (but incorrect) position.[55] This poor posture was discouraged in regular cavalry units. The Australian riders might not have been presentable for the Queen's Birthday Parade but they were able to ride with no instruction. They were essentially ready for action as soon as they were issued their horses.

The Australians did not invent the technique of mounted infantry; nor did they introduce it to the British who were already using it when the first Australians arrived in South Africa. Interestingly, mounted infantry was already part of the force structure of the Australian states prior to the beginning of the war, whereas it was a wartime contingency for the British. Labeled as "Light Horse," the Australian mounted infantry was considered to be the best of the Australian forces.[56]

Light Horse regiments were organized into traditional cavalry organizations of squadrons and troops. A regiment roughly equated to about 400 men in strength and was commanded by a lieutenant-colonel. Each regiment was further subdivided into three squadrons, each commanded by a major. Squadrons, lettered A, B, and C, were formed by three troops, each of eight sections. Troops were commanded by lieutenants. Sections, the basic organization of the Light Horse, were composed of four men, one of whom was the section sergeant.[57]

Because the Australian units were piecemealed to British units, it became difficult to identify actions as specifically Australian. Nor were the British liable to give credit to the Australians very readily.[58] This piecemealed organization of units limited the effect the Australians contributed. Had they worked under their own commanders in larger units (regiments, brigades, or divisions) they might have had a greater cumulative effect on operations. As it was, most of the Light Horse units served in squadron sized elements within larger British formations.

The natural tactical ability of the Australians to move using the terrain to their advantage, ride well, and conduct operations in irregular fashion made them a dangerous adversary to the Boers.[59] The British were quick to recognize the strengths of the Australian soldiers but they were unable to implement a program that could reproduce such results as it was due to cultural differences. The British soldiers were products of an urbanized and developed country. Contrasting their background to that of the Australians, the British came from a country which had been settled for hundreds of years, not a century. Their homes were the villages, towns, and cities of England, not the ranges of the outback. British soldiers depended less on their abilities to survive in an undeveloped country than their Australian counterparts who depended upon the horse and their innovativeness to live off a largely undeveloped land. In short, the cultural traits made the British and Australian soldiers so much different that to train the British soldiers to be like the Australians would have been nearly impossible without a great expenditure of time or effort.

The British would have eventually won the Boer War without the Australians using their persistence and modified tactics. Outnumbering the Boer fighting men about eight to ten to one, destroying the base of support provided by the Boer settlements, and running them to ground with mounted forces would have eventually triumphed.[60] The large number of Australians certainly helped end the war sooner and on terms more favorable to the British. Of the more than 15,000 Australians that served in South Africa, the majority were combatants, and, of these, all were eventually mounted. This gave the British commander in South Africa a tremendously improved capability to fight the Boers in mobile warfare where rapid movements over extended distances were used.

In terms of character, the Boer War highlighted some major differences between the Australians and British in the leadership and methods of conducting operations. Conservative dogmatism exhibited by the officers of the British Army not only caused high casualties in their own forces but gained the reproach of the Australians. The Australians demonstrated the flexibility of mind in the conduct of their tactics. Instead of using the horse mounted units in cavalry fashion, that is, in massed charges, the Australians roamed the veldt in loose, dispersed order. [61] A premium was placed on Australian initiative which allowed soldiers individually, or in small groups, to move from the direct control of their officers. This was antithetical to the tactics of the British which required the officers to maintain strict control of their soldiers. The result was the method employed by the European armies of the day, tight, linear formations.

Ironically, the Australians were following a common doctrine cited in the 1884 <u>Regulations for Mounted Infantry</u> for British and Colonial troops. This manual was a British War Office manual and specifically instructed the use of dispersed, "loose" order for field movements.[62] The need to travel in non-compacted formations was recognized fifteen years before the war in South Africa. It seems highly unusual that the Australians were able to immediately implement this doctrine whereas the British were not. If dispersed order was ordered for use in a manual, the need for it must have been recognized. Failure to use it was a violation of a tactical technique existing in British doctrine.

The strength of the Light Horse not being drilled as regular cavalry and moving in extended order cross country was more a reflection of the Australian's natural abilities than any particular schooling. Open order depended upon instinct and initiative to work as a unit. It was characteristic of men who had worked the grasslands of the outback.[63]

The Australians were pragmatic in their approach to fighting the Boers and used whatever worked, even to the point of using the same tactics the Boers used. Raids, ambushes, and infiltrations became common methods of fighting for the Australians who displayed an ability to improvise where the manuals left off. [64]

The effects of the Boer War on the Australians was not as profound as it was on the British however. The Australians' tactics depended on initiative and flexibility. They quickly adapted to the situation and fit their methods to the particular environment at hand. Not bound by tradition, they were prone to disregard doctrine if it did not work and adopt other methods.

Likewise, the doctrine for mounted infantry prescribed a tactical technique which clearly fit their methods of operation as well as their individualistic nature. While the British infantry were still fighting in platoon mass, firing in volleys, the Australians were using the terrain and cover and firing as individuals. Although they shared a common doctrine, they applied it completely differently. Not until the war had progressed for a number of months did the British gradually begin changing their methods.[65]

The experience of the Australians with the British in the Boer War also served to provide an appreciation for how the British operated. The Australians came away with disdain for the British officers and their general methods of operation. No doubt the highly controversial and emotional courts-martial and execution of Captain "Breaker" Morant and another Australian officer of the Bush Veldt Caribineers did much to flavor future Australian opinion of the British.[66]

The disdain the Australians shared for the British commanders resulted from the continued practice of conventional massed tactics after repeatedly suffering catastrophic losses to the Boers. What caused the Australians to scorn the British methods can be partly attributed to the makeup of the forces involved. The Australians sent to South Africa were volunteers with a very small corps of professional officers. Essentially they were former militia and volunteer unit members that signed on for overseas duty. They embodied Australian characteristics that made them fiercely independent. The Australian soldiers were collectively intolerant of incompetence, a trait exhibited by a number of the British senior commanders during the beginning of the Boer War.

Probably the most important influence of the Boer War

on the Australians was in the political realm. The war provided the common bond between the separate states. It also provided a tradition for the new Australian Army and satisfied a patriotic nationalism. At all levels it assured the Australians that their abilities were a match for the best that the British had.

The Results of the Boer War on the British Cavalry and Australian Mounted Infantry

The central tactical lesson of the Boer War eluded them. The reason for those humiliating reverses was not the marksmanship of the Boers, nor their better guns or rifles, nor the crass stupidity of the British generals, all myths which British people found it convenient to believe. It was that the smokeless, long range, high velocity, small bore magazine bullet from rifle or machine gun, plus the trench, had decisively tilted the balance against the attack and in favour of the defence."[67]

The effects of the Boer War on the Australians confirmed their organizations and doctrine. It validated the importance of horse mounted troops, especially mounted infantry armed with the rifle. The Australian method of fighting as an extention of their heritage was confirmed. The "loose order" formalized in British mounted infantry regulations was only an instinctive part of the Australian way of riding. The success of the mounted infantry caused Australians to increase the number of units in the militia prior to WWI.

Australia became a nation as the Boer War was being fought in South Africa during 1901. It took the next few years for the Australian Army to evolve. As part of consolidation of the army in 1903, the individual states relinquished administrative controls over their respective units. Of importance was the amalgamation of the state forces into the Commonwealth in January 1903 providing for a centralized command and control of the Australian Army. A common doctrine for the Australian forces similar but separate from that of the British Army was written. For mounted forces the new doctrine was contained in the 1902 <u>Mounted Service Manual.</u>[68]

Horse mounted forces proved their importance in South Africa. Twenty three regiments of Light Horse were formed between 1903-1914 as a direct result of their successes during the Boer War.[69] The Light Horse units were formed under a variety of names but had the essential ingredients of mounted infantry. Original names included units such as the New South Wales Lancers, the Queensland Mounted Infantry, the Bush Veldt Carabineers, and the Victoria Mounted Rifles. Names like "Mounted Rifles" or "Mounted Infantry" implied that the units were rifle equipped. The New South Wales Lancers were a lance equipped Light Horse unit; however, they discarded their lances for rifles during the Boer War.

Whatever their titles were, they were identified in the 1902 Australian regulations as either "mounted infantry" or "light horse." By 1915 the distinction between Australian Light Horse, mounted infantry, and lancer units was in name only.

The 1902 Mounted Service Manual specified the roles of Light Horse and mounted infantry differentiating between the two in that Light Horse was required to perform traditional cavalry tasks such as reconnaissance as well as fight as infantry. Mounted infantry was to use the horse as a means of mobility in order to yet to the fight but it was not required to perform any other specialized tasks using the horse.[70]

The Australian mounted infantry entered the war in South Africa equipped with rifles as their primary weapons. Dismounted employment was the norm. The Australians left the war still armed with the rifle and the knowledge that their tactics worked. The British cavalry entered the war armed with the carbine, lance, and sword; it left the war armed with the rifle and sword. The rifle became the primary arm by regulation.[71]

The British cavalry finally transitioned to the weaponry which would allow them to fight dismounted, the rifle. Their doctrine was validated. The importance of dismounted action against a rifle equipped foe was driven home by the irregular Boers. The sword and lance proved to be entirely inappropriate against guerillas and dug in Boers protected by barbed wire.

The British had formed mounted infantry units as a subsequent means to improve their tactical mobility but maintained their cavalry as well. The British mounted infantry followed the 1884 and 1899 regulations for mounted infantry which required the use of tactical dispersion. British cavalry maintained the disciplined formations used prior to the war and were infrequently able to employ the massed charge. When the British cavalry was able to charge the few times it did, it was successful against a largely dispersed and disorganized enemy. Charges against entrenched Boers proved to be both difficult and costly.

The transition of the British cavalry armament was the result of the experiences gained fighting rifle equipped Boers. The Australians had always subscribed to the use of the rifle by mounted troops and their tactics reflected this. As mounted infantry, they rode to the battlefield, dismounted, and fought as regular infantry with rifle and bayonet.

Perhaps the Australian decision to standardize the rifle was a result of budget. Both regular infantry and mounted infantry were equipped with the same rifles. The foresight of Australian officers to equip their mounted forces with a weapon of suitable range paid dividends in South Africa. For whatever reason, the rifle became the primary arm of the British cavalry by regulation and remained the primary arm of the Australian Light Horse by regulation and tradition.

Until the end of the Boer War, the British cavalry had been armed with the carbine. Much handier to use from the saddle due to its shorter length, the carbine suffered a correspondingly shorter range and accuracy than the rifle. The carbine was not issued to all types of cavalry and was only designed to supplement the primary arm, the saber or sword.[74]

The sword was found to be largely useless in South Africa against the Boers who frequently used guerilla tactics and were not good targets for massed charges. Instead, the Boers used their superior marksmanship and longer range of their rifles to stand off and shoot carbine equipped cavalry which was unable to effectively respond. The result of the lessons learned was the standardized issue of the rifle to all British cavalry following the war. The Australians were able to validate their use of the rifle and their mounted infantry tactics against the Boers. As a result, both the rifle and tactics remained essentially the same after the war.[75]

Between the Wars

The roles of the two Australian mounted elements of mounted infantry and Light Horse merged between the Boer War and WWI. This merger probably occurred for two primary reasons. The first reason might have been the requirement for reconnaissance and security. Since the Australians fought as part of a larger British Commonwealth force, an abundance of traditional cavalry (Yeomanry) was normally available in South Africa to fulfill the traditional cavalry roles of reconnaissance and security. This division of tasks between the cavalry and Light Horse prevented a duplication of effort and allowed the Light Horse to concentrate on their primary responsibility of fighting dismounted as infantry.

The other reason was that the requirements for Light Horse and mounted infantry explicitly stated that they both be able to fight dismounted. With this duplication of tasks, it would be very easy to have one type of mounted force to do both "Light Horse" and "mounted infantry" work.

The only thing left to do was standardize the name for both as "Light Horse." Instead of two elements semantically different, their missions were merged along with their names. Light Horse units retained the attributes of mounted infantry as their primary function. They would fight dismounted as infantry and use the horse as a means of mobility on the battlefield. By the beginning of the First World War, the Light Horse units provided an important part of the Citizen Military Forces in Australia and were considered to be some of the very best.[74]

In the traditions of not maintaining a large standing

army, the Australians reverted to their citizen forces system and a small permanent military establishment after federation in 1902. Two key factors played a role in determining this mix of forces, economics and the success of a similar system at the outbreak of the Boer War whereby the bulk of the overseas forces came from voluntary enlistments.

Voluntary overseas duty was a result of statutory limitations on the employment of the militia outside of Australia. It forced the army to quickly adapt another solution to the home service militias when war was declared in August of 1914. Volunteers were called upon to supply the manpower required to field a force for overseas deployment. The Australian militia men were very young cadets or young men who had transitioned to the Citizen Military Forces (C.M.F.) due to universal military training after the Boer War.[75] To prevent sending such a young force to war, the Australian Imperial Force (A.I.F.) was formed separately from the militia and was completely composed of volunteers older than the junior C.M.F. for service outside of Australia.

There was a large number of C.M.F. members who met the minimum age requirements transferred to the A.I.F. Additionally, those who joined gave the army an excellent foundation of men experienced in basic military skills. Many of the senior leaders of the A.I.F. came from the regular forces initially, providing both experience and continuity.[76]

Post-Boer War modifications to the Australian Army standardized the separate state operations and tactics. A corps of permanent cadre with a mix of both regular infantry and Light Horse units were formed. By 1914 there existed approximately 9,000 men in the Light Horse regiments. These units were considered some of the best soldiers of the nine brigade peacetime army.[77] Considering the cost and trouble of training horse mounted troops, 9,000 was a considerable number for a small army. The proven utility of such troops obviously played a major role in their retention after the Boer War.

Light Horse regiments were not formally brigaded nor trained as parts of brigades or larger organizations until mobilization. This was difficult due to the dispersion of the territorially aligned, non-regular forces, composing the Australian Army. Some regiments were designated for independent assignments to infantry divisions as the divisional reconnaissance elements. For example, the 13th Light Horse Regiment was designated as a divisional unit and was the only Australian Light Horse regiment to serve outside the Middle East during World War I.[78] The result of this limited large unit training meant that Australian officers had very little experience commanding or staffing such units when the First

World War broke out.

The training of professional army leaders prior to World War I was standardized with the establishment of the Royal Military College at Duntroon, near Canberra, in 1911. Although only able to graduate a small number of officers prior to the First World War, their impact was regarded as substantial by Australian commanders during the initial days of the war.[79] Officers already serving prior to the establishment of Duntroon prepared themselves professionally by home study or by attending British or Indian Army service schools. Limited exchange programs allowed Australian Army officers to serve with various units and staffs to gain experience in the British Army.[80]

A large number of officers of the A.I.F. would come from the ranks of the militia units, advancing by proven ability during the war and bringing credit to the leader selection system used by the Australians.

The Boer War served as a training ground for the Australians prior to the First World War. It provided the leadership of the future Australian regiments, divisions, and corps valuable experience. This experience was to stand the Australians in good stead in the years to come, especially in the Middle Eastern theater of war.

Since all of the Australian forces in the Boer War were

eventually mounted, all the Australians with Boer War experience had to have had mounted experience. The success of the horse mounted infantry during the Boer War was not lost on the Australians who validated their doctrine and organizations. This key aspect of their military heritage certainly affected the large number of Light Horse regiments organized and retained during the inter-war years.

NOTES

    1.   R. L. Wallace, The Australians at the Boer War (Canberra: The Australian War Memorial and the Australian Government Publishing Service, 1976), p. 350.

    2.   Russel Ward, The Australian Legend (Melbourne: Oxford University Press, 1958), p. 212; Gordon Greenwood, ed., Australia, A Social and Political History (New York: Frederick A. Praeger, 1955), p. 225.

    3.   A. L. McLeod, The Pattern of Australian Culture (Ithaca, N.Y.: Cornell University Press, 1963), pp. 14, 23.

    4.   Ward, The Australian Legend, P. 10.

    5.   John Laffin, ANZACS at War (London: Abelard-Shuman Ltd., 1965), p. 23.

    6.   H. S. Gullett, The Australian Imperial Force in Sinai and Palestine, 1914-1918 (Sydney: Angus and Robertson, Ltd., 1923, p. 213.

    7.   Ward, The Australian Legend, p. 215.

    8.   Robert Hughes, The Fatal Shore (New York: Vintage Books, 1986), pp. 322-326.

    9.   McLeod, The Pattern of Australian Culture, p. 320.

    10.   Ward, The Australian Legend, p. 1.

11. McLeod, The Pattern of Australian Culture, p. 18.

12. Laffin, ANZACS at War, p. 23; A. J. Hill, Chauvel of the Light Horse (Victoria, Australia: Melbourne University Press, 1978), p. 35. The British officers in both the European theater and in the Middle East complained that the Australians were "undisciplined" because they did not salute. Chauvel explains that the complaints surfaced during the wars with Kruger and were still being made when the Australians were fighting Hitler. A part of the Australian military heritage, failure to salute did not equate to discipline as understood by Australians. The outstanding battle record of the Australians is used as a case in point.

13. Ward, The Australian Legend, p. 19; Eliot Cohen and John Gooch, Military Misfortunes: The Anatomy of Failure in War (New York: The Free Press, 1990), p. 156.

14. Peter Firkins, The Australians in Nine Wars (New York: McGraw-Hill Book Company, 1971), pp. 80-81.

15. Firkins, The Australians in Nine Wars, p. 58.

16. Patsy Adam-Smith, The ANZACS (West Melbourne: Thomas Nelson Australia Pty. Ltd., 1978), p. 170.

17. "The Wonderful Waler, Warhorse Supreme," Australian Horse and Rider, November 1975, p. 8; Mike Cummings, "Harking Back, The Australian Light Horse,"

Hoofs and Horns, November 1984, pp. 44-45.

18. "The Wonderful Waler, Warhorse Supreme," Australian Horse and Rider, November 1975, p. 8-9.

19. Philip Warner, The British Cavalry (Melbourne: J. M. Dent and Sons, Ltc., 1984), p. 187.

20. A. J. Hill, Chauvel of the Light Horse (Victoria, Australia: Melbourne University Press, 1978), p. 42. Chauvel as a small boy rode to and from boarding school, a couple of days and many miles from his *home.* Not uncommon in his time, boys were encouraged to ride.

21. Laffin, ANZACS at War, p. 17.

22. Hughes, The Fatal Shore, P. 103.

23. McLeod, The Pattern of Australian Culture, p. 23.

24. Laffin, ANZACS at War, p. 17.

25. L. L. Robson, The First A.I.F.: A Study of It Recruitment, 1914-1918 (Hong Kong: Silex Enterprise and Printing Co., 1970), p. 13; Brian B. Lewis, Our War: Australia During World War I (Melbourne: Hogbin, Poole (Printers) Pty. Ltd., 1980), P. 17.

26. McLeod, The Pattern of Australian Culture, p. 23.

27. Ward, The Australian Legend, p. 17.

28. "The Australian Army: A Brief History,"

(Canberra: Australian Government Publishing Service, 1983), p. 2.

29. Laffin, ANZACS at War, p. 17.

30. "The Australian Army: A Brief History," p. 6.

31. Hill, Chauvel of the Light Horse, pp. 7-10.

32. Firkins, The Australians in Nine Wars, pp. 5-6; Laffin, ANZACS at War, p. 18.

33. "The Australian Army: A Brief History," p. 4.

34. Ibid., p. 6.

35. Robson, The First A.I.F.: A Study of Its Recruitment.

36. Laffin, ANZACS at War, p. 23.

37. Wallace, The Australians at the Boer War, p. 300.

38. Thomas Pakenham, The Boer War (New York: Random House, 1979), p. 610.

39. Michael Sarthorp, The Anglo-Boer Wars, (Poole, U. K.: Blandford Press, 1987), pp. 11-12.

40. Ibid.

41. Bruce I. Gudmundsson, "A Lesson from the Boers," Military History Quarterly, Vol. 1, No. 4 (Summer 1989): 34-35.

42. Barthorp, The Anglo-Boer Wars, p. 59.

43. Brereton Greenhous, Dragoon: The Centennial

History of the Royal Canadian Dragoons, 1883-1983 (Ottawa, Canada: Campbell Corp., 1983), P. 75.

44. Michael Barthorp, British Cavalry Uniforms Since 1660 (Poole, U.K.: Blandford Press, 1984), pp. 150-157.

45. Pakenham, The Boer War, p. 610.

46. William Weir, "Advantage Sought On High Ground," Military History, August 1986, P. 37.

47. Firkins, The Australians in Nine Wars, P. 10.

48. Greenhous, Dragoon: The Centennial History of the Royal Canadian Dragoons, 1883-1983, p. 80; Pakenham, The Boer War, p. 327; Major G. Tylden, Horses and Saddlery (London: J. A. Allen and Co., 1965), pp. 221-222.

49. Firkins, The Australians in Nine Wars, p. 9; Pakenham, The Boer War, p. 260.

50. Hill, Chauvel of the Light Horse, p. 9.

51. Firkins, The Australians in Nine Wars, p. 9.; McLeod, The Pattern of Australian Culture, p. 15.

52. Laffin, ANZACS at War, p. 23.

53. Hill, Chauvel of the Light Horse, p. 20.

54. Wallace, The Australians at the Boer War, p. 300. One Australian recorded his feelings of Yeomanry horsemanship as follows: 'It is good fun to see the Imperial Yeomanry ride, as they fall off at the rate of one a minute.'

55. Joan Starr and Christopher Sweeney, Forward:

The History of the 2/14th Light Horse (Queensland Mounted Infantry) (Queensland, Australia: University of Queensland Press, 1989), p. 5 (photo section).

56. William Johnson Halloway, M.P., Advanced Australia: A Short Account of Australia on the Eve of Federation (London: Methuen and Co., 1899), p. 183; Firkins, The Australians in Nine Wars, p. 55.

57. Greenhous, Dragoon: The Centennial History of the royal Canadian Draaoons, 1998-1983, p. 80; Hill, Chauvel of the Light Horse, p. 47.

58. Wallace, The Australians at the Boer War, p. 332; Firkins, The Australians in Nine Wars, pp. 8-9. This issue became a serious point of contention in every war. The Australians felt slighted for not receiving their fair share of the commendations and awards until they made it an issue.

59. Ian Jones, The Australian Light Horse (Sydney: Time-Life Books, 1987), p. 8; Wallace, The Australians at the Boer War, p. 60.

60. Major J. W. Woodmansee, ed., "Keeping the Peace," History of Revolutionary Warfare, Vol. 4 (USMA, West Point:

Department of History, 1971), p. 30. The British forces eventually reached a ratio of about ten to one in South Africa. As they have found in modern insurgencies using guerrilla warfare, a minimum of about eight to one is required in military forces to win. In cases such as Malaya in this century, they massed almost 24:1 if civil police authorities are counted also.

61. Field Service Manual, Mounted Infantry (London: War

Office, 1884), pp. 21-22.

6 2. Ibid., p. 22.

63. Cohen and Gooch, Military Misfortunes: The Anatomy of Failure in War, p. 156.

64. Pakenham, The Boer War, p. 572; Laffin, ANZACS at War, p. 23.

65. Firkins, The Australians in Nine Wars, p. 15.

66. Arthur Davey, ed., Breaker Morant and the Bushveldt Carbineers (Capetown, South Africa: Van Riebeeck Society, 1987), p. ix.

67. Pakenham, The Boer War, p. 610.

68. John Laffin, The Australian Army at War, 1899-1975

(London: Osprey Publishing, 1982), p. 8.

6 9. Ibid.

70. Laffin, ANZACS at War, p. 51.

71. Barthorp, British Cavalry Uniforms Since 1660, p. 150; Pakenham, The Boer War, p. 483.

72. Mike Chappell, British Cavalry Equipments,

1800-1941 (London: Osprey Publishing Ltd., 19830, p. x.

73. Barthorp, British Cavalry Uniforms Since 1660, p. 150.

74. James D. Lunt, Charge to Glory (New York: Harcourt Brace and Co., 1960), p. 187; Firkins, The Australians in Nine Wars, p. 55.

75. Robson, The First A.I.F.: A Study of Its Recruitment, 1914-1918, p. 76.

76. Hill, Chauvel of the Light Horse, p. 48.

77. Laffin, The Australian Army at War, 1899-1975, p. 8.

78. J. M. Brereton, The Horse in War (New York: Arco Publishing Co., Inc., 1976), p. 137.

79. Hill, Chauvel of the Light Horse, p. 43.

80. Ibid., p. 45.

CHAPTER 2 - WAR IN THE EASTERN THEATER

Horse Cavalry and Mounted Infantry: British Yeomanry and Australian Light Horse

> Yeomanry and mounted rifles are cavalry soldiers, enlisted or enrolled as such, who are trained to use the rifle as their principal offensive or defensive weapon. . . . By mounted infantry is meant fully trained infantry, mounted solely for purposes of locomotion. Such troops are not to be regarded as horse soldiers but as infantry possessing special mobility.[1]

When war was declared in August 1914, the Australians immediately offered their services to the Commonwealth effort. A tremendous surge of patriotism produced volunteers in numbers so large that men were initially turned away by the Australian forces. The first volunteers for overseas service were quickly trained, equipped, and prepared for movement to Europe.

Initial Australian troop deployments by November 1914 included an infantry division and a brigade of Light Horse. Both were meant to be sent to Europe to fight but a report regarding the substandard camp arrangements in England forced the Australians to winter over in Egypt.[2] This stay in

Egypt proved to be a fortuitous decision for the Australian Light Horse units. Had they continued on to England and France, they might have spent the better part of the war, as did many other Western cavalry regiments, waiting miles behind the lines for action, or, dismounted and used as filler infantry on the Western Front. As it was, they were presented a chance never again to be repeated for horse mounted units of the Western armies.

It was in this regard that the British kept their regular cavalry regiments in Europe and sent the Yeomanry to the Eastern theater. The Yeomanry units were composed of citizen soldiers much as the Light Horse units were. Rural farmers and countrymen filled the ranks while the officers, unlike the Light Horse, were traditionally aristocratic. The Yeomanry had never enjoyed the status of the regular cavalry but they saw themselves as a step above the other arms and branches.[3]

The supreme irony of this situation was the fact that the units that were originally thought to be less than suitable for combat on the Western Front were to fight some of the greatest mounted actions in modern history. The regular line cavalry units in Europe were the ones that were to spend the war dismounted behind the lines. Only a few units were able to participate in the exploitation phase of the July-November 1918 Allied offensive in Europe. The rest waited patiently for their turn. In the end, the Eastern Theater became the example cited by cavalrymen around the world as the classic campaign of mounted warfare. It was the Eastern Theater that provided the Australians a unique chance to demonstrate their initiative and flexibility on a large scale.

When the first Australian units reached Egypt in November 1914, they were retained due to the milder climate and to provide additional security for the Suez Canal. Turkey's entry into the war in October 1914, threatened the Suez Canal. In February 1915, the British changed their war plans and the Australians were kept in Egypt pending an operation to land at Gallipoli in Turkey. The majority of Light Horse units deployed to Gallipoli as infantrymen, leaving their horses in Egypt.

During the campaign in Gallipoli from March to December 1915, the front along the Suez Canal was relatively quiet. It was not until the return of the forces from Turkey to Egypt that the combined Turco-German forces attempted to seriously threaten the Suez Canal defenses. After the evacuation of Gallipoli in December 1915, the majority of the Australian infantry was sent to the Western Front leaving almost all of the Light Horse units in the Middle East. The remaining Light Horse were the core of the mounted forces that fought in Sinai and Palestine.

It was not until the Australian units arrived in France and Egypt in December 1915 that the Australian commanders were able to make a substantial impact upon the conduct of operations. Until the end of the Gallipoli campaign in December 1915, the highest Australian command was divisional. This meant that only tactical decisions at the lower levels could have been made by Australian commanders.

At Gallipoli the divisions were very limited in the ability to affect large scale operations. There was no room for maneuver and division commanders only had to manage very limited tactical matters. The Australians were afforded little chance to demonstrate their initiative at the higher command levels until after Gallipoli. Two Australian officers received corps commands.

Of the two corps commanded by Australians (one in Europe the other in the Middle East), the one in the Middle East, The Desert Mounted Corps, is of particular interest to this study. The Desert Mounted Corps was the largest tactical mounted force commanded by a single commander in Western history. The corps' actions are of interest in regards to both its tactical and subsequent operational employment in the final battle of the war in the Eastern Theater. The corps consisted of Australian, New Zealand, Indian, and British mounted troops. This provides an interesting comparison of forces and a view of the entire force whose actions were flavored by their Australian commander.

The Australian Approach to War, 1914

Your training manuals are as much use to the Australians as the cuneiform inscriptions on a Babylonian brick.
-Colonel Bridges, Australian Staff Representative to the Imperial General Staff[4]

While the Australians and British had generally entered the First World War with a fairly common doctrine for mounted forces, their applications were vastly different. The British had learned a great deal from the Boer War in the tactical application of cavalry and had officially sanctioned many positive changes to their equipment and tactics.[5] While they seemed to understand the implications of the changes due to the methods of warfare and technology used in South Africa, they had difficulty incorporating the essence of the changes. The changes were not institutionalized. While regulations and manuals cited the new tactics of dispersed order based upon lessons of the Boer War, cavalry commanders continued to train much as they had in the past for massed mounted attacks.

For example, the rifle had proven to be superior to the carbine for mounted work. The "boot to boot" mounted charge had generally proven to be unsuitable against Boer guerillas or prepared defenses with modern arms in South Africa even though circumstances sometimes allowed for successful charges to occur. And, despite the emphasis of marksmanship in the new manuals, the traditions of the cavalry were retained in the training for the charge. Even the lance returned to the cavalry inventory after an absence of only seven years.[6]

This seeming inflexibility demonstrated by the British cavalry was in stark contrast to that of the Australians who were willing to adapt to the situation as required. The background of the Australian leadership and their soldiers was less dependent upon traditions than it was on a pragmatic approach to the solution of a problem. The doctrine for mounted infantry had proven correct under the circumstances in South Africa. The Australians continued to follow the doctrine which had been developed with the British. Dispersed order and the reliance on the rifle for dismounted work maintained their importance. The failure of the British to embrace the changes to their own doctrine after the Boer War became a major point of contention with the Australians.

Especially after the Gallipoli campaign in 1915, the Australians were extremely critical of British inability to adjust and change in respect to new situations. Lack of imagination, a leadership crippled by old age and traditions, and a seeming disregard for the lives of the soldiers, characterized the

Australian perception of the British officer corps.[7] These perceptions were, more often than not, reinforced on a regular basis to the Australians who were subject to the failings of their higher British commanders and staffs. The tremendous casualty rates incurred by British insistence on using outmoded tactics soured the relations between the two forces even more.

While the Australians continued to develop their doctrine in light of what was learned in South Africa, they practiced what they learned. When they went to war in 1914, the Australian Light Horse were as prepared to fight a modern war of mobility as they were in 1899 South Africa. The Australians could hardly have guessed the effects of barbed wire on the mobility of horse mounted units. Since the closing with the enemy in the charge was not an Australian technique of mounted combat, barbed wire was only a minor concern. The Australians could dismount and fight as infantry, thereby negating the effect of barbed wire on a massed horse mounted charge.

The Australians validated their techniques and small unit tactics by using dispersed order against the Boer opponents. Contrast this to the British who fought in their traditional massed formations. The British only modified their tactics late in the Boer War to "open order" after suffering a number of defeats. Although a number of British leaders recognized the problems, innovative changes to affect the solutions were not generally welcomed in a system which promoted and rewarded unquestioned conformity.[8]

The Australians accepted the expediency of a system which appointed leaders over them. They still demanded that the leaders be able to prove themselves worthy of their positions by virtue of their ability and not artificial designations such as rank. The antipathy of the Australians towards appointed officials, which went back to colonial times, translated to the methods of selection of the leaders in the military.[9]

The Australians approached the conduct of war as a natural outgrowth of their experiences and culture. The dislike for authoritarian leadership and dogmatic approaches to the conduct of operations led them to develop their own style of fighting. This fighting was modeled on what worked.

Placed in an environment which was similar to that of their own country, the Australian Light Horse were able to excel in warfare which required their skills of mounted activity combined with their ability for living on the land. Their successes in South Africa presaged their exploits that were to follow in a similar vein during the First World War.

The Mounted Forces in the Eastern Theater

The organization of the A.I.F. in the Egyptian

Expeditionary Force (E.E.F.) underwent a number of changes during the time it arrived in Egypt in 1915 until it ended the war in Syria in 1918. The units most affected were the Light Horse regiments. As the regiments arrived in Egypt they had been organized into war time brigades. Brigades normally consisted of three regiments and those regiments which were left over were assigned "detached" duties such as reconnaissance elements for the infantry divisions along the Suez Canal.

By the time the Light Horse units returned to Egypt after the Gallipoli campaign, the status of the horse on the battlefield in Europe had drastically changed. Cavalry units had lost their utility on the European battlefields due to a number of factors. The Western Front featured barbed wire obstacles, massive bomb and shell craters, and weapons that kept the horses so far from the front lines that they were unable to exploit even major successes. The horse cavalry became an apparent anachronism.

The situation in the Middle East was markedly different from that experienced by cavalrymen in Western Europe. The differences in the terrain, the relative massing of forces on a smaller frontage, the massing of tremendous indirect firepower, the shell pocked landscape, the vegetation surrounding the battlefields, the tremendous obstacle system emplaced when the war became static, and the machinegun all combined to create situations completely different from the Middle East.

The Influence of Terrain

The difference in terrain was a major factor between the Middle East and European theaters of war. In Europe, the variety of the terrain differed every few kilometers. In the main area of operations for the belligerents in France, the terrain was characterized by the woods and hills of eastern France to the relatively level swamps of northwestern France and Belgium. This condition existed only during the early days of the war before the terrain was rendered unrecognizable by the constant shelling in the battle areas. While the terrain generally favored cavalry operations in the central portion of the theater early in the war, it was mostly for smaller operations of squadrons and perhaps regiments.

In most of central Europe the wooded areas generally are found on the upper parts of the hills as the valleys provide the arable land. A well developed road net favored mounted operations as the quality of the numerous unimproved roads was suitable for horses. The valleys offered the possibility of mounted action as they were generally cultivated and cleared of obstacles. The Europeans rarely fenced their land which made access for horse mounted units very easy.

Cavalry units could use the extensive road network to

move rapidly about the countryside, mass, and conduct tactical operations in the open countryside. The strength of horse cavalry units was its relative mobility on all types of terrain which was not too thick with vegetation. So, while the roads were important, they were not absolutely necessary.

The roads provided a route through the more heavily wooded or vegetated areas of European terrain and, therefore, assisted the mobility of the cavalry. The more densely wooded terrain hindered quick movement and in the early days of WWI were avoided by infantry as much as the cavalry as it tended to make the command and control of units more difficult. Photographs from the era show infantry still using mass formations that should have been discarded after the Russo-Japanese and Boer Wars but remained as a tribute to tradition. However, these formations were only suitable in open terrain.[10]

Wooded terrain was not a good area to employ mounted units for several reasons. Not only did it break up the compact mass of horses necessary for a successful charge, it slowed the horses down. This made the mounted cavalryman an easier target for infantry sited in the woods. The trees, in effect, provided natural obstacles to the mounted units which prevented them from closing with the enemy effectively using one of the primary characteristics of cavalry formations, shock action. Wooded areas were therefore traditionally considered unconducive to cavalry operations and were avoided when possible.

Unlike previous wars, the massing of troops along the entire front from the North Sea to Switzerland caused another problem. During the "race to the sea" in the early days of the war, a nearly continuous line of troops was established along the terrain which best supported the movement of large armies. Only in those areas which were in swampy lowlands, or, in the mountains, were non-continuous lines formed. These areas were more lightly held by outposts due to the difficulty of negotiating the restrictive terrain. Obstacles and fortifications were built along the areas of troop concentrations. These served to prevent traversing by mounted forces. Since exposed flanks were rarely formed, the mounted forces were unable to be employed without first having an initial penetration of enemy lines.

The ascendancy of the defense during the early months of the war only exacerbated the problem for the cavalry. The answer to the failure of ground maneuver to breakthrough the enemy's defenses caused both sides to rely more on indirect firepower. The constant bombardment of a concentrated area of land literally transfigured the terrain.

Shell holes became obstacles in themselves. The constant churning of the soil blew away the topsoil and plant life. After a few good rains, the land was transformed and these conditions very quickly halted the use of the cavalry in any serious work near the front lines.

Large numbers of cavalry units were kept active on the Western Front during the war in hopes that they could be used to conduct the expected exploitation once the infantry broke through the initial enemy defenses. If the infantry was able to open a gap in the defenders' lines, the cavalry could pour through and race into the enemy's rear. This had been the dream of every cavalry commander. This situation was called "looking for the 'G' in 'Gap.'"[11]

Cavalry forces were used to conduct exploitations due to their superior relative mobility and speed. Able to outpace the infantry, mounted forces could race into the depth of the enemy's defenses and disrupt the continuity of the enemy's forces. The problem encountered by the cavalry on the Western Front was not solely the effects of modern weapons on cavalry. The biggest problems were the obstacles such as barbed wire, shell pocked ground, and the deep mud in the destroyed landscape. It was a combination of these conditions and the modern weapons which made the use of horse mounted cavalry temporarily obsolete.

The conditions by themselves were significant since the cavalry depended upon its tactical mobility to conduct operations. Combined with the weapons of improved lethality, the terrain and environmental conditions became an overwhelming problem for the horse cavalry. The horse cavalry quickly became a burden on the armies since they were not able to be used in the front lines and consumed tremendous amounts of supplies.

The massive obstacle belts emplaced by opposing sides prevented the movement of the horse mounted forces on the European battlefield. Senior commanders of both armies thought that the stalemate was only a temporary aberration and that a great breakthrough could easily be effected by greater mass and firepower. Cavalry would be kept behind the lines for the expected exploitation and subsequent pursuit whenever it was to occur. The bulk of the British regular cavalry units were sent to France to fill the perceived need for these forces.

What actually happened is that British cavalry forces sat out the majority of the war miles behind the front lines in France. By the time the Australians returned to Egypt from Gallipoli in late 1915, the reality of the Western Front had been established. Static trench warfare and the predominance of the defense over offensive movement and maneuver was the new reality of modern warfare in Europe.

The factors which prevented the use of cavalry in Europe did not exist in the Middle East. For these reasons, the mounted troops of the Light Horse were kept in the E.E.F. where they would be of use against the unfriendly Arab tribes, such as the Senussi, and the Turkish threat to the Suez Canal.

One common denominator affecting the operations of both the Australian and British mounted forces of the E.E.F. was the harsh terrain. The entire area of operations of the E.E.F. fell within the desert areas of the eastern Mediterranean. The theater of war ran from the Suez Canal through the northern Sinai, then northeastward through Palestine and Syria. The primary areas of operations lay relatively close to the coast of the Mediterranean Sea and were dictated by key terrain known as "hods" (oases) and rail lines. Only late in the campaign did the armies move inland. This move was possible only because of the availability of water sources.

Terrain affected operational maneuver of both sides (that is, the armies or corps conducting major operations at corps level or above). The arid climate restricted large movement of troops away from available water sources. The sources of water for the British lay near the coast in the Sinai where a major pipeline was built to support the movement of the army across the northern desert.[12] The actual topography of the land favored the employment of mounted forces much more than that of the western European terrain. Large open areas, unhindered by heavy vegetation and with generally good traffic ability for both men and animals, except in the sand dunes of the northern Sinai, provided an excellent area to deploy mounted troops.

The Mediterranean Sea generally acted as a protected flank for opposing sides while the desert forced limited operations on both. Unlike the Western Front in Europe, both tactical and operational maneuver were geographically restricted in the Middle East. On one side lay the sea, but on the other lay an area that neither side could profitably use unless the water sustenance problem could be solved.

In Europe, the opposing sides were faced by almost continuous lines of troops behind major obstacle systems from the North Sea to the Swiss Alps. In the desert, however, the flank was left open since neither side could obtain the necessary water to move large units through the desert to take advantage of the other's flank.

Return From Gallipoli

In early 1916 Australian infantry units were stripped from the Suez Canal defenses and sent to Europe. By the middle of 1916, the only Australian units remaining in Egypt were Light Horse. While the E.E.F. was stripped for filler units to replace those depleted on the Western Front, the commander of British forces in Egypt, General Sir Archibald Murray, requested that the Australian Light Horse units remain to defend the Suez Canal.[13]

Mounted training resumed for the Light Horse units that returned from Gallipoli and the men had a chance to reacquaint themselves with their horses. Some Light Horse units went without horses until new ones could be shipped from Australia. These dismounted Light Horsemen trained to fight as dismounted infantry.

One of the brigades, the 4th Australian Light Horse, was not to receive its horses for a year after its return to Egypt from Gallipoli. Composed of the 4th, 11th, and 12th Light Horse Regiments, the 4th Brigade was the only unit of the Light Horse to have practiced cavalry charges under its former commander, Lieutenant-Colonel "Dad" Forsyth. Forsyth had assumed command of the brigade prior to its departure from Australia. An avid horseman and cavalry romantic, Forsyth had wanted to make his brigade the image of the well disciplined British cavalry. He trained his troopers in close order drill and charging with drawn bayonets in lieu of swords. Forsyth was promoted and transferred after Gallipoli, but there were a number of veterans remaining in the brigade when it returned to Egypt that remembered the charges conducted in training.[14]

Along with the Light Horse in Egypt, the British War Office had transferred a number of Yeomanry regiments to the Middle East to fill the gaps left by the departing infantry. Horse cavalry units in Egypt were not constrained by the problems facing their brethren in Europe. In fact, the conditions were much more favorable for the employment of horse mounted forces since the terrain generally favored mounted movement and the massing of forces. Defensive positions were not established in a continuous line across the battlefield leaving exposed flanks. Since the situation had stabilized along the Western Front, it was decided that the Yeomanry could best be employed in Egypt. Thirty six Yeomanry regiments were sent to the Middle East, a majority of those mobilized.[15]

Theoretically, the training for the Yeomanry and Light Horse was supposed to be very similar. Since they were both armed with the rifle, the method of employment was virtually identical by the manual published in 1912. However, since the Yeomanry managed to keep their swords after the Boer War, their British commanders felt a compunction to practice with them.

Even though the rifle was the primary arm of both the Light Horse and the Yeomanry by regulation, the traditions of the cavalry were difficult to discard. Therefore, the Yeomanry spent time in mounted close order drill perfecting the formations and tactics that would lend themselves to a mounted charge. These tactics had been useful against poorly armed natives during the nineteenth century. They had not been used successfully against a modern, well armed enemy. The Yeomanry would have one last chance against natives.

After the entry of the Ottoman Empire into the war, the Arab Senussi tribe of Western Egypt was encouraged to rebel against the British rule in Egypt. The Senussi posed a serious internal threat to British control in Egypt. If the Turks could sponsor an armed insurgency among the Moslem Arabs, they might force the British to fight in two directions along the Canal. The Turks could then exploit these uprisings by pushing a strong force through the Sinai to capture the Suez Canal.

The British dealt with the Senussi tribe very quickly by sending a cavalry force to rout them from their hold in the Western Desert. In a brief engagement, the Yeomanry charge dispatched the lightly armed Senussi and killed their tribal leader. This ended the threat from one of the strongest Arab tribes.

The fight against the Senussi threat to the Suez Canal concluded with one decisive engagement in which a Yeomanry squadron charged with swords. This was the first successful mounted charge of the British in the Middle East during World War I. It was also conducted with considerable advantage to the Yeomanry. The Senussi were neither dug in nor armed with an abundance of modern weapons. The terrain was open and generally level, therefore favoring mounted action.[16] It was against tribes such as the Senussi that the British cavalry excelled in using its disciplined mass and shock action. The British cavalry had been training for and conducting such operations against lightly armed natives since the end of the Crimean War, and notwithstanding the lessons of South Africa, Yeomanry were suited for such battles.

The majority of Light Horse regiments continued to train as they had done since the Boer War, that is, to ride to the battle, dismount and fight. The lessons of the Boer War had only made a superficial impact on a number of British cavalrymen, however. While the British cavalry doctrine espoused the importance of the rifle, the traditional minded cavalry officers seemed to consider the sword as the weapon of choice. The British continued to train for the mounted charge.

The charge against the Senussi occurred when the same effect might well have been achieved by rifle fire. The charge covered a very short piece of open ground from a position in defilade.[17] The fact that the British did not try to engage the Senussi by fire, but chose to charge, demonstrates the strength of the cavalry tradition. Additionally, it emphasizes the cavalryman's assertion that the effect of shock action cannot be achieved by dismounted action. While this assertion might have been true under specific circumstances, the risks for losses are also not as great if a good position in which to fire from is achieved.

The weapons and equipment for the Light Horse was similar to that used by the British cavalry. The standardization and equipping eased the burden of logistics and training. The saddle was the British Pattern 1912.[18] Other accoutrements varied according to serviceability and the likes and dislikes of the Australians. The Australians, in their typical way, supplemented the regulation British cavalry mess kit and replaced it with a very serviceable "quart pot and billy" used by the horsemen in the outback. Both served as cooking and eating ware, holding more generous portions than the mess kit. The quart pot provided a boiling container not matched by issue gear and was used to prepare tea.[19]

The cavalry rifle bucket used by the Yeomanry was not used by the Light Horsemen until the end of the war. Instead, the Australians slung their rifles over their backs. Both the Light Horsemen and the Yeomanry were armed with the British designed Number 1, Mark III, Enfield Rifle which was first produced in 1907.[20] The Australians produced their own copy at their arms plant in Lithgow, Australia, and the rifles used interchangeable parts and ammunition.

The one item of equipment common to both the Yeomanry and the Light Horse which proved to be of importance was the ubiquitous horseshoe case. The case held extra horseshoes and doubled as an attachment for the cavalry sword which hung off the near side of the saddle. The Yeomanry used the horseshoe bayonets on their belts and were not issued swords until 1918.

Mounted Operations 1916 - January 1917

> The truth is, that Cavalry can and will fit its tactics to any country.[21]

The defense of the Suez Canal was a definite drain on the war effort in Europe, but necessary to protect the sea lines of communication from East Africa, India, and Australia. Because many of the experienced infantry units were sent to France to counter the main threat of the German Army, the horse mounted forces provided the most efficient solution to the economy of force mission in the Middle Eastern Theater. The terrain facilitated the movement of mounted forces freely constrained only by water supply. This made mounted forces desirable in lieu of infantry to cover the long distances.

Although the Turks attempt to effectively bring the Senussi into the conflict in 1916 failed, they still conducted a campaign to seize the Suez Canal. The Turco-German forces in Palestine made an effort to force a crossing of the Suez Canal in February 1916 after a march across the northern and central Sinai.[22] This campaign also failed but did prompt a halt to the reduction of British forces in the Eastern Theater.

General Murray determined that the best defense for the Canal was to push forward into the Sinai as far as possible and deny the water sources to the Turks attempting to approach the Suez Canal. In the spring of 1916, the Light Horsemen began operating to the east of the Canal conducting raids, reconnaissance, and conventional offensive operations as regiments and brigades. The Australian and New Zealand Corps (ANZAC) Mounted Division was formed at this time with three Light Horse brigades, numbered 1-3, and the New Zealand Mounted Rifle Brigade.[23]

In April 1916, the 9th Light Horse Regiment struck towards the center of the Sinai in a raid. In the early morning of 15 April 1916, they attacked a Turkish well drilling unit and destroyed the equipment and well. This created a significant problem for the Turks since the approach from Gifgafa was the only way to the Suez Canal from the central Sinai.[24] By destroying the water source at Gifgafa (also known as Bir el Jifjafa or Jifjafa), the Australians forced the Turks to use the only feasible alternative approach along the narrow coastal avenue in the north. The ease by which the Australians were able to approach Gifgafa with mounted forces apparently discouraged the Turks from pursuing the central approach afterwards. Later in April, the Turks attempted another attack on the Canal. They pushed a column along the northern track towards Kantara (also known as El Qantara or Qantara).

Kantara was important as a rail terminus on the east side of the Canal and a pumping station for the water lines being built along the northern Sinai coast. Both water and rail lines had been built by Murray's directive toward the villages of Oghratina and Katia (also known as Qatiya) in early 1916. Murray's intent was to further develop the small oases and rail stops as bases for further operations against the Turks in Palestine. [25]

General Murray had subdivided the effort for the defense of the Suez Canal by assigning geographic areas to forces, and by placing all troops east of the Canal under the command of a subordinate, General Lawrence. Lawrence commanded a corps sized unit known as the "Eastern Force" which consisted of several British infantry brigades grouped into divisions and the mounted forces of some Yeomanry and Light Horse regiments.[26]

Major-General Harry Chauvel commanded the ANZAC Mounted Division. Chauvel was an Australian regular who had served his entire career in mounted infantry units. Beginning as a subaltern in the Queensland Mounted Infantry, he served in South Africa with distinction. Known to be an outstanding horseman and avid rider, Chauvel had been made the brigade commander of the first Light Horse Brigade to arrive in Egypt. He took his Light Horsemen to Gallipoli as dismounted infantry, was promoted to division commander, and returned to Egypt at his own request to serve with the Light Horse again.[27]

Chauvel had made an excellent reputation for himself among his countrymen at Gallipoli where his cool determination and quick decisions saved lives and the situation during a major Turkish attack on Australian lines.[28] A reserved and quiet man, he never gained a reputation as a popular commander, but he was well respected by all with which he worked.

When Chauvel learned of the Turkish advance towards the Canal in April, he ordered the 2nd Light Horse Brigade to Kantara from its positions along the Canal for possible employment as a reserve. The Turks struck the forward outposts of Katia and Ohgratina inflicting heavy losses on the British Yeomanry and routing them westward through Romani. The Light Horse quickly moved up and filled the gap with two brigades. Lawrence, to whom the ANZAC Mounted Division was subordinate, committed what was the first in the series of mistakes regarding the employment of the Light Horse.

Instead of keeping the Light Horse massed for a move against the flanks of the Turks or in reserve for a counterstroke, Lawrence detached the 1st and 3rd Brigades from Chauvel and spread them among British units employing them piecemeal. Lawrence parceled some of the mounted units of the Light Horse out to British infantry divisions to use as divisional cavalry.

The dispersal of the Light Horse units among divisions to be used for cavalry missions was an error. It was an accepted tactic of the day to assign cavalry squadrons or regiments to divisions. Lawrence failed to understand the difference between horse mounted infantry and horse cavalry however and used them interchangeably.

The 2nd Brigade and the New Zealand Mounted Rifles were left with Chauvel and employed in a defense-in-depth of Romani.

The attachment of the Light Horse to British infantry divisions was a poor application of mounted infantry. This employment fit the doctrinal methods for the employment of cavalry, but was not the best method of employing mounted infantry. The British use of the Light Horse in the reconnaissance and security roles was better suited to cavalry organizations such as the Yeomanry.[29]

The Yeomanry, armed and trained primarily with the sword, was better suited to conduct security missions, a traditional role of cavalry. The Light Horse had the primary mission to fight as infantry and was better trained for traditional dismounted infantry tasks. The British commander failed to grasp the essential differences between the two types of mounted forces and, therefore, did not exploit their potential capabilities.

The Light Horse could have been better used as a mobile reserve, or, as another maneuver element of the corps formation. A quick analysis of numbers shows that the regiment of Light Horse assigned to a British infantry division might hope to field about 300 rifles at best. This number accounts for every fourth man being a horse holder. In relative terms, this would have been an insignificant num number to contribute as a maneuver element in a divisional battle. However, had the regiments been kept brigaded, or, retained in a divisional organization instead of being dispersed, 900 (brigade) to 2,700 (division) rifles would have made a substantial maneuver element for a corps commander to employ on an enemy flank or rear.

The Turkish advance halted in its move toward Kantara and the forces under Lawrence conducted extensive patrolling and defensive preparations during May through July. The 1st and 3rd Light Horse Brigades were returned to Chauvel; however, the New Zealanders were taken away. The Turks continued to wait and build their supplies and strength east of Romani near Oghrantina during the summer.

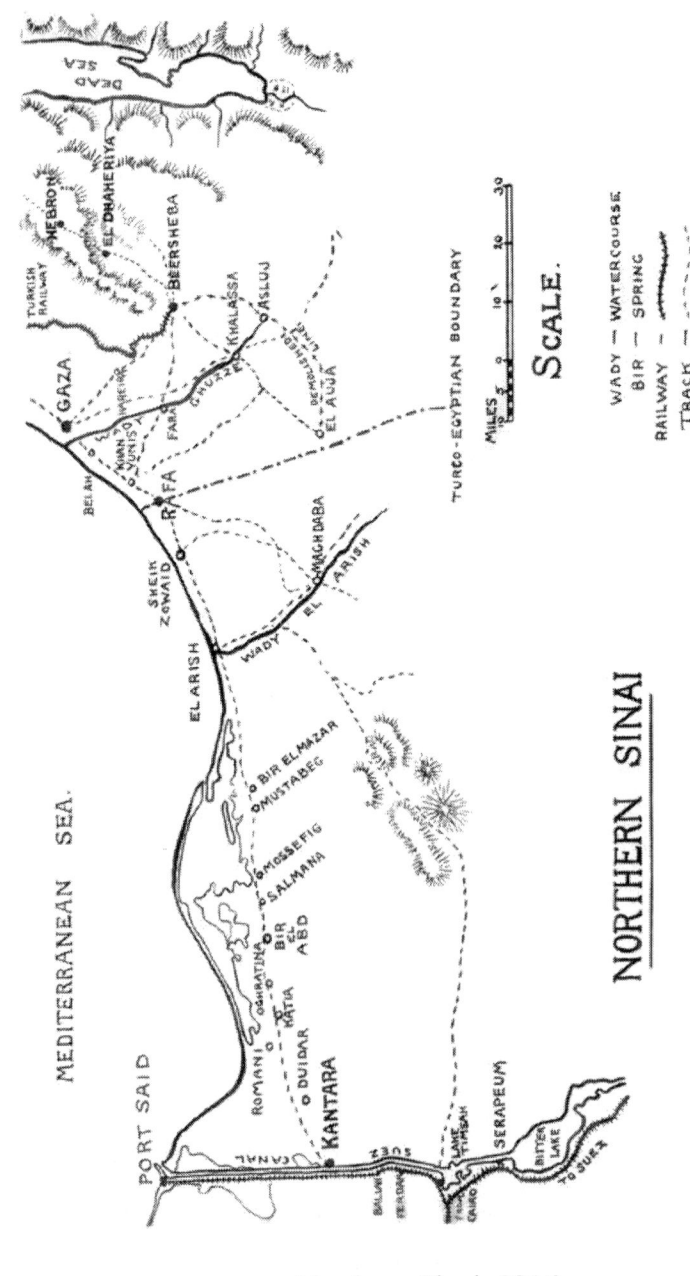

Northern Sinai, 1916

By August 1916 the Turks had been forced to completely abandon their move through the Sinai except along the coast of the Mediterranean. The destruction of their wells by the 9th Light Horse Regiment in central Sinai left them no other choice but to use the coastal approach into Egypt. By mid-summer the Turks here ready to mount a major battle to seize the British outposts in the north-central Sinai and move to the Canal.

Moving westward toward the Canal in a series of night movements to avoid the heat of the day and aerial observation, the Turks moved their forces forward in bounds. On 2 August 1916, the Turks attacked the outpost lines of the Australians near Katia. Forcing the Australian screen line back, the Turks marched on toward Romani. Romani was significant as the last railhead, water depot, and oasis before reaching the Canal from Palestine. Its capture could provide the Turks an excellent logistical facility for the final move toward the Canal, about 25 km away.[30]

The Turkish Army approaching Romani numbered about 20,000 men with supporting artillery. Their morale was high and many of the soldiers were veterans of the Gallipoli campaign. Overall, the ratio of opposing forces was approximately equal in the battle area of Romani. The Turks massed their forces in the southern portion of Lawrence's lines by conducting holding attacks along the northern part where the British infantry was stationed. The ratio of the Turks to the Australian Light Horse brigades was approximately 10:1.

The stage for the battle was chosen by Lawrence who endeavored to force the engagement on terms favorable to his forces. He established his defenses tied into the Mediterranean coast reasonably expecting the Turks to attempt to outflank his lines to the south which were open into the desert. Chauvel was given responsibility for conducting a screening action forward of the defenses of Romani initially. The 1st and 2nd Light Horse brigades were to provide the first line of defense as giving way under pressure of the Turkish advance from Katia.

Behind the Light Horse were two British infantry divisions deployed in a series of low hills running semi-circle around Romani to the eastern side. Tied into the coast on the left flank, the hills ran clockwise around Romani providing a modicum of key terrain on the approaches to the village. The infantry positions were relatively fixed and prepared whereas the Light Horse had no designated positions from which to fight.

General Chauvel's intent was to draw the Turks into the prepared positions around Romani by fighting a deliberate delay. By not preparing fixed positions around Romani,

Chauvel hoped to maintain operational security and prevent the Turks from discerning his plans.[31]

Chauvel was task organized with the 1st and 2nd Light Horse Brigades. The New Zealand Mounted Rifles, 5th Yeomanry Brigade and 3rd Light Horse Brigade were placed under the operational control of Lawrence during the initial part of the battle and were located about a half day's march west of Romani.[32] The terrain favored both mounted and dismounted action between Katia and Romani. On the immediate approaches to Romani the sand dunes inhibited both mounted and dismounted trafficability near Romani.

Chauvel's brigades formed the basis of the defense of Romani to the east. The 1st Light Horse Brigade was organized to defend on the main desert track to the east of Romani. The 2nd Light Horse Brigade conducted a screen initially, then a rearward passage, and was placed in divisional reserve.

The battle at Romani opened in the early morning hours of 3 August shortly after midnight and progressed throughout the day. Unable to reach the water supplies at Romani, coupled with the lengthening supply lines and intense heat of the Sinai summer, the Turkish attack culminated in the late afternoon of 4 August.

The battle was conducted in a classic mounted delaying action as Chauvel's Light Horse units gave ground, reformed dismounted, fought, and then moved mounted to new positions, trading space for time. By late afternoon, the Light Horse had reached a line of defense which could go no further back and hand-to-hand fighting developed among the Turks and the dismounted Light Horse. As Chauvel's division moved back towards Romani, the mounted troops were used to extend the defensive line into the desert. They blocked Turkish attempts to flank the main line of resistance. Eventually the line bowed back toward the southwest in a semicircle around Romani. The horse mounted soldiers were able to quickly shift their forces by thinning the lines and extending them outward on the open desert flank.[33]

Chauvel determined the location of the Turkish main attack on his right flank and employed the 2nd Light Horse Brigade to block the attack. The division's lines gradually grew to cover about one third more ground than when the battle began. The extension of the 1st Brigade and the employment of the 2nd Brigade on the open desert flank was made more timely by their mounted movement.

The first major battle of the Palestine campaign was fought largely by the Australian Light Horse Units of Chauvel's division. If nothing else, casualty returns show that the ANZAC Mounted Division was the most heavily engaged.[34] A major failure in corps level command and control left the 5th

Yeomanry Brigade largely out of action until near the end of the battle. By locating his headquarters far from the battlefield in Kantara (35 km away), Lawrence deprived himself of timely information and the ability to influence the battle with the forces he had reserved for his own employment, the 5th Yeomanry Brigade and the 3rd Light Horse Brigade.

Commanding the battle by telephone negated Lawrence's ability to see the battlefield both literally and figuratively. When the telephone lines were cut by artillery, control of the battle was completely decentralized to the division and independent brigade level.[35] It depended upon the initiative of the local commanders such as Chauvel.

The British infantry of the 42nd Infantry Division was located too far to the rear to influence the battle significantly. The 42nd was held in positions near Kantara and was only sent forward after determining the thrust of the Turkish main effort toward Romani. This essentially left them out of the fight during the most crucial period due to movement time forward. The other infantry division, the 52nd, was employed holding the left flank and was engaged by a Turkish supporting attack along an extended frontage.

The Turkish attack began to falter in the late morning of 3 August due to the lack of water and the intense summer heat. Chauvel astutely determined the demise of the Turks and continued to fix the forces to his direct front while further extending his lines into the desert in order to refuse his right flank. By using one brigade to fix the Turks and gaining relief of another Light Horse Brigade by local uncommitted British infantry, Chauvel could attempt to flank the Turks with a mounted brigade of Light Horse.

Without direction from Lawrence's headquarters, Chauvel immediately attempted to exploit the developing situation to his favor. He requested the assistance of a nearby British infantry brigade, yet uncommitted, to relieve a Light Horse Brigade in place. The British brigadier refused without direct orders from his commander which would take time to receive. The window of opportunity was only available for a limited time and the delay caused Chauvel to miss it.

Only a failure to cooperate by the local British infantry brigade commander prevented Chauvel's planned move from being a success. Without orders from the British infantry division commander, the British brigadier refused to assist.[36] Unable to replace his committed Light Horse brigade in the line caused a significant missed opportunity. This example clearly shows Chauvel's initiative and the inflexibility of the British commander.

With pressure to the front of the Light Horse brigades, Chauvel could not disengage and move to the flank without the assistance the British infantry brigade could have provided by fixing the Turks. While Chauvel attempted to gain assistance, the Turks began to withdraw, thus removing the conditions Chauvel had hoped to exploit in order to flank the attacking forces.

Even more interesting is the fact that the 5th Yeomanry Brigade arrived later to tie into the Australian right flank. This placed the 5th Yeomanry in an unprecedented location on the far left flank of the attacking Turks. Had the commander of the 5th Yeomanry considered, he might have easily swung around and struck the Turks in the exposed left flank. Instead, no indications exist that the 5th Yeomanry took the initiative on their own to perform such a maneuver. Instead, they remained on the defensive. One notable exception was a British squadron commander, who, on his own initiative, tied into the flank of the Australians. He was the exception, not the rule.

The Turkish attack was spent as a combined result of the summer heat, lack of water, and stiff Australian defense. While the scattered forces were reorganized and communications with Lawrence's headquarters reestablished, the Turks retraced their route toward Palestine and their water sources. The Australians and British prepared to conduct an exploitation with their mounted forces. The Turks skillfully withdrew towards Palestine by defending the limited water points necessary for operations by either side.

Early in the morning of 5 August, Chauvel was given command of all mounted forces and ordered to pursue the Turks. Only the 3rd Light Horse Brigade was initially in condition to carry out the mission since it had not been committed during the battle of Romani. The 3rd Brigade advanced about 15 km to the east and broke the Turkish left flank at Katia about mid-day on 4 August.

The 1st Light Horse Brigade, 2nd Light Horse Brigade, and the New Zealand Mounted Rifles advanced after reorganizing and replenishing. The 5th Yeomanry were brought up from the reserve. Chauvel knew the Light Horse troops were exhausted after constant fighting for almost two days in extreme summer heat but decided that the Turkish positions at Katia had to be destroyed by nightfall of 5 August. If not, his regiments would be unable to continue their advance for lack of water. Katia was the only source of water short of another day's march eastward and was key terrain for this reason.

The first attempted large scale mounted attack of the desert war occurred on the mid-afternoon of 5 August 1916. Chauvel decided to attack mounted into the Turkish positions located at Katia counting on the disorganization of the Turkish rear guard. He hoped to overcome resistance through the shock action of closing on the Turks before they could react. The

Light Horsemen fixed bayonets while still mounted and charged into an oasis of scrub, palms, and unseen coastal swamp. Their assault failed short of the Turkish positions because of the broken terrain and determined Turkish defense. The attack turned into a dismounted fight quickly as the Australians could not break through the trees and undergrowth of the oasis mounted. The action was broken off by Chauvel who then marched his exhausted force back to Romani.[37]

The terrain undid the mounted attack of the Light Horse brigades. Had the mounted attack succeeded, it might have been one of the major mounted actions of the war. As it was, the action at Katia reinforced the belief that mounted charges were no longer good tactical solutions. The terrain forced the Light Horse to dismount short of the objective and fight without the benefit of having pushed the attack home.

While the terrain was not in any way similar to that of Europe, it had the same effect on the horse mounted troops' mobility. The swamps and scrub undergrowth reduced the mobility and broke up the momentum of the mounted attack just as the shell craters, mud, and barbed wire did on the European battlefields.

Additionally, accounts show the Light Horse fixed bayonets while mounted. This indicates that the commanders had the intention of dismounting short of the objective in mounted infantry form. A rifle with a bayonet is extremely awkward to use from the saddle. It can therefore be assumed that the Light Horse had no intention of conducting an assault on horseback with bayonets fixed.

Although Katia was the first attempt to attack the Turks mounted, it is doubtful that a charge could have been consummated with bayonets affixed to rifles while the troopers were mounted. It did set the tone for future actions where mounted advances (attacks) culminating in assaults (charges) would be successful.

Chauvel took a risk but lost against the will of the Turkish infantry and the denseness of the palm scrub oasis which broke the momentum of the mounted action. The exhaustion of his soldiers, their lack of water, lengthening line of communications, and failure to capture the water of the oasis caused them to reach their culminating point. They were forced to abandon the exploitation.

Considering the fact that Chauvel's division was not the only mounted force on the field at Romani, his actions showed a tremendous amount of initiative and flexibility. Loss of contact with the next higher headquarters at Kantara did not affect his ability to act. On the contrary, he attempted to take advantage of the situation.

Lawrence, with two brigades of mounted troops under

his control, gave vacillating orders and failed to employ the mounted units efficiently. The 3rd Light Horse Brigade was entirely left out of the fight during the critical time in the defense. Lawrence ordered them to march and countermarch around in the desert during the 3rd of August when their assistance would have made a substantial contribution to the fight.[38] As it was, the 3rd Brigade arrived tired and required rest before it could assist in the exploitation of the retreating Turkish troops.

5th Yeomanry Brigade was in the best position to conduct a mounted attack into the flank or rear of the Turks but was constrained by Lawrence's poor appreciation of the situation. Instead, they arrived and tied into the right flank of Chauvel's Light Horse units playing only a minor role. While the commander of the 5th Yeomanry might have taken advantage of the situation he failed to. Even in the exploitation toward Katia on the 5th of August, the Yeomanry was in a relatively advantageous position to charge the Turkish rearguard but did not while Light Horse units attempted to in less availing circumstances.

The battle was certainly influenced by the mounted forces but it was not a mounted fight. The horses provided a relatively better degree of mobility to the defenders allowing them to displace and mass forces more quickly than the attacking Turks. It was to the advantage of the Light Horse to have the interior lines, thereby forcing the Turks to move further through the desert in order to flank the Australians.

What is particularly interesting about the exploitation and pursuit of the Turks to Katia is that the 5th Yeomanry Brigade was immediately available to conduct this action and did not. The mission for an exploitation and pursuit was traditionally a cavalry mission which would have been conducted by Yeomanry, not mounted infantry. It is only speculation, however, the commander of the Yeomanry might have still felt uncomfortable about the shortcomings of his units in the desert and therefore failed to press Lawrence to allow the 5th Brigade to exploit and pursue.[39]

Chauvel's failure to pursue was contingent upon two facts. First, his Light Horse units were exhausted from two days hard exertion in the Sinai summer. Many of the horses had gone unwatered for hours and needed to recuperate. Additionally, Lawrence did not regain control of the battle in a timely manner. The assignment of all mounted forces to Chauvel occurred after the Turks had already broken contact and moved to the East.

The position of the 5th Cavalry Brigade was qualitatively better since it had not taken part in the major part of the fighting and would have been in better condition for immediate use. In any case, the 5th Cavalry Brigade was given to Chauvel on 5 August and used in the initial pursuit of the Turks towards Katia as part of the Australian Mounted Division.

In the first major mounted action of the war in the Middle East, the forces of the ANZAC Mounted Division clearly stood out for their initiative and flexibility while those of the British showed a disappointing lack of these qualities. The ability to act had obviously been demonstrated at the lower levels as the charge against the Senussi by the Yeomanry proved. The abilities of the more senior commanders of the Yeomanry were tested and found to be lacking both in the earlier defeat at Oghratina, the battle of Romani, and finally the exploitation to Katie.

The conclusion of the battle at Romani and the subsequent exploitation marked the last phase of British defensive operations in the Eastern Theater. The remainder of the campaign placed the British forces on the offensive and the Turco-German forces on the defensive. For the time being, the E.E.F. was to be constrained by the logistical effort required to move fodder and water forward in stages from the Suez Canal.

The respite from continuous pursuit allowed the Turco-German forces to prepare defensive works along the approaches from the Sinai into Palestine. At Maghaba in

December 1916, and Rafa in January 1917, the Light Horse encountered prepared positions on dominating terrain generally not suitable for mounted charges Hard fought dismounted actions were required to capture the positions which were dug in and well sited.

The battle at Maghaba was largely a fight conducted by the ANZAC Mounted Division against the entrenched Turkish garrison. Again the Light Horse units attempted to charge the Turkish positions and nearly succeeded in overrunning several trench lines in hastily executed mounted drives.

The lack of good assault positions close to the Light Horse objectives which could provide close in cover to the trenches caused the charges to be aborted in all but a couple of small actions. Beginning as much as 3,000 meters away, one regiment was able to close to about 1,200 meters before it received accurate machine gun fire. This caused the regiment to seek cover and halt the mounted charge.[40] Subsequent action by the regiment was dismounted.

In one instance, a troop of the 10th Light Horse Regiment was able to leap the trenches. In order not to be caught in enfilading fires, the troop kept going. It was followed shortly thereafter by a squadron which succeeded in charging and clearing the trench.[41] These charges, the first successful ones by Light Horse against prepared positions, were a matter of last minute decisions and opportunities presented by the situation, not deliberately planned actions. Although the terrain was conducive to mounted actions and obstacles did not hinder closing with the enemy by mounted action, commanders still had planned to ride within small arms range, dismount, and assault as infantry using the terrain to their advantage.

In this respect, the tactics of the Light Horse had not changed. It does demonstrate the presence of mind and flexibility of the Australians under the circumstances. The charges, while not planned, were opportunities offered by the situation of which the Australian leaders took advantage.

At Rafa, on the Egyptian and Palestinian borders, the actions of the Light Horse reverted to mounted infantry actions due to the nature of the terrain and the relative strength of the enemy defenses. The Turkish positions were largely sited on high ground unsuitable for charges. The dominating positions and excellent fields of fire prevented closing on the trenches in mounted assaults.

Entry Into Palestine: The Gaza Battles

By early 1917, the supply lines of the E.E.F. had progressed to the point which allowed the radius of operations to expand out of El Arish (west of Rafa), one of the last major towns in the northern Sinai outside of Palestine. Murray's next objective became Gaza, a fairly sizable town enroute to

Jerusalem by way of the Sinai coast. As a communications hub, Gaza had a rail station and was the focal point for a number of desert tracks which radiated to the north, south, and east to towns like Beersheba.

Gaza was important to the Turco-German forces for a number of reasons. As a coastal town, it had inadequate port facilities but it was the terminus of the rail line from Jerusalem. Astride the historical avenue of approach into southern Palestine, Gaza occupied significant terrain features that made it key.[42]

From the coast at Gaza, running roughly southeasterly, a series of ridges connected with the town of Beersheba to form a natural defense against south-north movement. Several dominating ridgelines outside of Gaza had been heavily fortified and prevented access to the town from the south. Additionally, cultivated fields and hedgerows of cactus restricted movement to the narrow roads into the town. Lastly, the Mediterranean Sea on the western side of the town prevented an approach from that quarter by land forces and only with great difficulty by marine borne forces.

Murray not only needed Gaza because of its significance in dominating the approaches into Palestine, but also for its use as a forward depot to continue offensive operations against the Turks and Germans. El Arish was too far from the borders of Palestine to allow easy transfer of supplies forward. El Arish would be unable to support such operations and therefore a new logistics base was required. The rail facilities in Gaza would be beneficial for transloading supplies well forward. Additionally, operations would have to move further from the coast as the E.E.F. advanced north. The battle to seize the town was planned for March 1917, about the time required to finish moving supporting assets forward out of El Arish.

    The plan included the use of the mounted troops to surround the town and interdict movement in or out. Murray had secured the addition of more mounted troops from the War Office which was pleased with the conduct of the campaign in the Sinai. The additional mounted units allowed for the creation of another mounted division. The newly formed Imperial Mounted Division was formed from one British cavalry and two Australian Light Horse brigades.

    With the ANZAC Mounted Division, the Imperial Mounted Division was to swing wide and surround the town of Gaza preventing the escape of the defenders and reinforcement by reserves. This mission was very suitable for mounted forces as it made the best use of the speed and cross country mobility. The mounted units had the capability to quickly envelop the town before the enemy could organize a contiguous defense in the gaps. Infantry divisions were to reduce the town with the assistance of the mounted units which would attack the town from the flanks or rear if necessary.

It might have been easier to attempt to bypass Gaza had the Turks not held the necessary water wells in the desert around the town. The Turks also held a number of defensive positions along the ridges adjoining Wadi Gaza running southeast into the desert at Beersheba. The Turkish defensive line was constituted by a series of trenches and fortifications which were backed by reserves. Beersheba was the last point in the fixed defenses which ran almost 50 kilometers. Forces to the east of Beersheba consisted only of small pickets of Turkish cavalry and patrols.[43]

Bypassing the defensive lines completely would entail a major move through the desert by the British away from water supplies absolutely necessary for the conduct of any major operations. Under the best of conditions, horses require about eight gallons of water a day. In desert conditions, during the hot season, the requirement for water increases depending upon the work involved and the temperatures.

Murray determined that he could not support such an option such as a mounted envelopment of Beersheba with the logistical base in El Arish and limited watering stations through the desert. The wells in the desert had only minor capacities. It would do no good to break through the enemy defenses between Gaza and Beersheba for the same reasons. It was decided to attack directly against Gaza and force the Turks back in a frontal action.

The attack on Gaza was scheduled for 25 March 1917. Initially, the mounted troops of the Imperial Mounted Division were able to encircle the town and reach the coast in the north. A tragedy of errors violating the principle of war now known in U.S. military parlance as "unity of command" and slipshod communications caused the attack to go awry. Poor synchronization between the artillery and the commanders delayed the attack. Originally meant to begin in the early morning, the attack did not begin until it was past noon.[44]

All surprise was lost and the Turks and Germans put up stiff resistance. Ironically, the plan was time phased and even though it had begun almost six hours too late, the phasing was never adjusted. About the time the troops were making their greatest successes, the commander of the attacking British forces, General Chetwode, incorrectly assessed the situation and ordered a withdrawal. The fact that the town was literally captured and the key facilities destroyed by the retreating Turks was known to Chetwode who adamantly ordered that the attack broken off.[45]

The town, whose capitulation was guaranteed, was

therefore handed back to the bemused Turks and Germans who had a chance to analyze their errors and fix the defenses. The German commander, General Von Kressenstein, immediately used reinforcements from the quiet eastern sectors, to strengthen the line between Gaza and Beersheba. To the Light Horsemen, this turned into one of the bitterest ironies of the entire war. It tainted their opinion of the senior British commanders even more.[46]

Murray decided to attempt a second attack on Gaza in April. The E.E.F. supply lines were pushed forward to within a few kilometers of the front, siege artillery brought forward, and for the first time in history, tanks were introduced to warfare in the Middle East.[47]

On 17 April 1917, the Light Horsemen of the ANZAC Mounted Division moved out to the eastern flank of the army with a mission to intercept reinforcements sent to Gaza. They would have to break through or infiltrate the main defensive line and move to the north and northeast of Gaza in order to interdict the routes into the town, much as they had done in March.

The two mounted divisions of the Desert Column were unable to move to a location suitable for mounted action and, when the major action began on 19 April, were unable to use their speed and mobility to their advantage. Instead, the newly formed Imperial Division ordered its horsemen of the Yeomanry Brigade, 3rd, and 4th Light Horse Brigades to dismount out of small arms range and conduct bayonet attacks. The dismounted troops suffered very heavy casualties from artillery and machine gun fire as they attempted to close on their objectives.[48]

The second battle for Gaza ended in tragic failure for the E.E.F. Casualties were not only high but debilitating to morale. The traditional meat grinder tactics reminded many of the Australian soldiers of the Gallipoli campaign and the ineptness of the British commanders willing to sacrifice their soldiers.[49] It certainly did not suit the Australian method of fighting. The static warfare tactics of frontal assault against fortified positions failed to maximize the capabilities of the horse mounted forces. The successes gained in the Sinai by the Australians had fueled their desire to fight a war of mounted maneuver where a premium on initiative and improvisation were the keys to their victories.

NOTES

1. <u>Yeomanry and Mounted Rifle Training, Parts I and II, 1912</u> (Warrington and London: Mackie and Co., Ltd., 1912), P. 1; "The Palestine Campaign," Fort Riley, KS, The Cavalry School, 1922-1923, p. 66.

2. Hill, Chauvel of the Light Horse, p. 45.

3. Gullett, The Australian Imperial Force in Sinai and Palestine, 1914-1918, p. 81; Lunt, Charge to Glory, pp. 187-188.

4. Firkins, The Australians in Nine Wars, p. 19. Comment by British Colonel (later, Major-General) Bridges, future commander of the Australian forces. Killed leading the Australian division at Gallipoli.

5. Mike Chappell, British Infantry Equipments, 1908-80 (London: Osprey Publishing Ltd., 1980), p. 8.

6. Barthorp, British Cavalry Uniforms Since 1660 (Poole, U.K.: Blandford Press, 1984), p. 149.

7. Firkins, The Australians in Nine Wars, pp. 57-58.

8. Ibid., p. 16.

9. Ward, The Australian Legend, P. 1.

10. John Terraine, The Great War, (New York: The MacMillan Company, 1965), p. 87.

11. Cavalry, produced by Robert Toner, John Keegan's series Soldiers, 55 min., British Broadcasting Company, London, 1985, videocassette.

12. David L. Bullock, Allenby's War: The Palestine-Arabian Campaigns 1916-1918 (London: Blandford Press, 1988), pp. 22-23.

13. Gullett, The Australian Imperaial Force in Sinai and Palestine, 1914-1918, p. 52.

14. Ibid., P. 59.

15. Lunt, Charge to Glory, p. 188.

16. Ion L. Idriess, The Desert Column (Sydney: Halstead Printing Co., Ltd., 1932), p. 117; Cyril Falls, Armageddon: 1918 (The Nautical and Aviation Publishing Company of America, 1964), pp. 5-6.

17. "The Palestine Campaign," Fort Riley, KS, The Cavalry School, 1922-1923, pp. 276-277.

18. Ross Macalpine, "Australian Military Saddles," Horse Mounted Detachment, Parramatta Barracks, Parramatta, Australia, 1987, p. 60.

19. Jones, The Australian Light Horse, p. 23.

20. W. J. B. Smith, Small Arms of the World (New York City: Gallahad Books, 1973), p. 251.

21. Bullock, Allenby's War: The Palestine-Arabian Campaigns 1916-1918, p. 142.

22. Jones, The Australian Light Horse, p. 47.

23. Bullock, Allenby's War, p. 24.

24. Major T. H. Carley, O.B.E., With the Ninth Light Horse in the Great War (Adelaide: The Hassell Press, 1924), pp. 33-38.

25. Bullock, Allenby's War, p. 28.

26. General Sir Edmund H. H. Allenby, The Advance of the Egyptian Expeditionary Force (London: His Majesty's Stationary Office, 1919), p. 39.

27. Hill, Chauvel of the Light Horse, p. 66.

28. D. M. Horner, ed., The Commanders (Sydney: George, Allen and Unwin, 1984), p. 65; Gullett, The Australian Imperial Force in Sinai and Palestine, 1914-1918, p. 228; Hill, Chauvel of the Light Horse, p. 56.

29. W. B. Fraser, Always a Strathcona (Calgary, Canada: Comprint Publishing Co., 1976), p. 56.

30. Lieutenant-General Sir George MacMunn, Military Operations Egypt and Palestine. Maps - no other information on carton.

31. Colonel Kirby Walker, "The Palestine Campaign," Part I, Fort Riley, KS: The Cavalry School, 1921, p. 11.

32. Lieutenant-General A. P. Wavell, The Palestine Campaign (London: Constable and Co., Ltd., 1928), PP. 47-50.

33. Gullet, The Australian Imperial Force in Sinai and Palestine, 1914-1918, pp. 157-163.

34. Ibid, p. 184; Jones, The Australian Light Horse, p. 54.

35. Captain 0. Teichman, The Diary of a

Yeomanry M.O. (London: T. Fisher Unwin Ltd., 1921), p. 74.

36. Ibid.; Horner, the Commanders, p. 70; Firkins, The Australians in Nine Wars, P. 84.

37. Idries, The Desert Column, p. 135; Gullett, Tie Australian Imperial Force in Sinai and Palestine, 1914-1918, p. 171.

38. Carley, With the Ninth Light Horse in the Great War, pp. 43-44.

39. Gullett, The Australian Imperial Force in Sinai and Palestine, 1914-1918, p. 81.

40. Ibid., pp. 219-220.

41. Ibid., p. 223; Starr and Sweeney, Forward: The History of the 2/14th Light Horse (Queensland Mounted Infantry), p. 100.

42. Jones, The Australian Light Horse, p. 60.

43. Cyril Falls, Military Operations Egypt and Palestine From June 1917 to the End of the War, Part I (London: His Majesty's Stationery Office, 1930), Map 12; Bullock, Allenby's War: The Palestine-Arabian Campaigns 1916-1918, p. 44.

44. Wavell, The Palestine Campaigns, p. 81; Bullock, Allenby's War: The Palestine-Arabian Campaigns 1916-1918, pp. 44-46.

45. Jones, The Australian Light Horse, p. 62.

46. Gullett, The Australian Imperial Force in Sinai and Palestine, 1914-1918, p. 294.

47. Jones, The Australian Light Horse, p. 63.

48. Hill, Chauvel of the Light Horse, p. 108.

49. Jones, The Australian Light Horse, p. 65; Lewis, Our War: Australia During World War I, Dust Cover.

CHAPTER 3 - LIGHT HORSE C

Battle for Beersheba

> It was one of these incidents, seemingly trivial, which in truth determines the fortunes of campaigns . . . .[1]

As the result of the poor showing of the E.E.F. at Second Gaza, General Dobell was relieved. General Chetwode was moved to replace his former commander, General Dobell.[2] Chauvel was promoted to the rank of Lieutenant-General and advanced to the position of corps commander. Murray's headquarters remained in Cairo so that any improvements in the resulting command structure were probably coincidental at the higher levels. Significantly, Chauvel became the very first Australian to command a corps.

Chauvel's command was reorganized and included the ANZAC Mounted Division, the Australian Mounted Division (formerly Imperial Mounted), the Yeomanry Mounted Division and the Imperial Camel Corps Brigade. The name of the corps was changed from Desert Column to the Desert Mounted Corps (D.M.C.).[3]

While this reorganization was taking place, the remaining units of the 4th Australian Light Horse Brigade, had fought dismounted since Gallipoli, finally received their replacement horses. A number of soldiers still remained from the originals that had landed in Egypt in 1915.[4]

After the battle of Second Gaza, General Chetwode, who was subordinate to Murray, now commanded all the forces east of the Suez. Chetwode proposed a plan to envelop the Turkish lines at Beersheba and roll up the defenses towards Gaza. The limitation on the plan was purely logistical. Lack of water sources in the desert meant that water supplies would have to be brought forward. This option would be extremely time consuming and risky.

The Turks controlled the wells at Beersheba. These wells were sited on the only major source of water in the region. The underground system of springs flowing to Wadi Gaza fed into the wells at Beersheba. The town contained at least seventeen well sites. [5] Allied possession of the town and wells was key to successful operations in the area and an essential location from which to continue operations out of the Negev north towards Jerusalem.

The plan to attack the exposed flank of Beersheba with the mobile D.M.C. was a major operation for the E.E.F.[6] Within context, it was an attack into the Turkish center of gravity for the defense of the Gaza - Beersheba line. If Beersheba fell, the road through Hebron to Jerusalem would be open. Also, Beersheba was an important supply and water point in the Negev for the Turkish Army. Beersheba was the last point in which garrisons could be maintained in the desert. The Turkish defenses were anchored on Beersheba for this reason.

Beersheba lies in a shallow valley (Wadi Gaza) which leads out of the hills to the Mediterranean Sea. The valley runs east-west and with the surrounding hills, forms a natural impediment to north-south movement. The hills to the north of the town and those to the south overlook the approaches and were considered dominating terrain. The terrain is largely unvegetated and consists of hard packed sand with gravel. The terrain favored both mounted and dismounted traffic ability.

The main avenues of approach into the town were the six roads and tracks radiating out from its center. The major approaches were evenly distributed with three to the north and three to the south of Wadi Gaza. The roads and the area adjacent to them generally provided good avenues of approach and maneuver areas as they followed the natural course of the terrain through the most trafficable areas. The gradual slope of the terrain to the south of Beersheba provided little or no concealment to an attacking force which had to traverse as least five kilometers of open ground before reaching the town.[7]

Only Beersheba had the necessary source of water to supply units as large as a mounted corps. Capture of Beersheba would collapse the continuity of the Turkish defensive line and provide the water from the large well complex. The positioning of the E.E.F. in Beersheba would protect the flank of a force moving along the Phillistine Plain next to the Mediterranean coast by denying the wells and base of operations to the Turks.

The use of the infantry to outflank Beersheba was discarded due to their slower rate of movement and the fact that they would arrive at the objective area exhausted from a long cross country march. The benefit of the mounted envelopment was the speed of the march which provided the advantages of operational security (less chance of detection by being in the area less time) and the ability to deliver the troops to the objective area in condition to fight.

The Turco-German forces were confident after the first two battles of Gaza that they could continue to hold the line against the E.E.F. Logistics would become the major problem of the British. The German commander, General von Kressenstein, was certain that the British could not solve the water problem easily.

In a story of its own, a classic deception plan was instituted to make the Turco-German forces commander, von Kressenstein, believe that the E.E.F. would feint against Beersheba but attack Gaza as the main effort again. Remarkably, the German commander accepted the deception plan which included a map case with a fake letter dropped intentionally in front of a Turkish patrol. The letter detailed the move against Beersheba as only a feint and the main attack against Gaza. In actuality, In actuality, the main attack was planned against Beersheba and the feint was against Gaza.[8]

Ismet Bey, commander of the Turkish garrison in Beersheba, never accepted the deception. Instead, he continued to strengthen the defenses by entrenching the garrison on the outskirts of the town, fortifying key terrain on approaches from the southeast, and preparing the key installations and wells for demolition.[9]

Von Kressenstein did not believe that the British could move a large force to face Beersheba without being detected due to the accompanying logistical effort required to support the forces in the desert. If such a plan were attempted, the Turkish and German forces could use their interior lines to quickly reinforce the garrison. Speed was therefore a key element in the execution of the British plan.

All the initial plans for the offensive were conducted under the auspices of Murray, who, despite his professionalism and attention to detail, fell prey to the political machinations at the War Office in London. After the second failure at Gaza, the Imperial General Staff had made plans to replace Murray. A suitable replacement was found in General Edmund Allenby (later knighted), a cavalryman. On 27 June 1917, the War Office had Allenby replace Murray.[10]

Allenby was an experienced soldier who had commanded a squadron in the Boer War and was quick to adopt the plan envelop Beersheba with a mounted corps. His own experiences in the Boer War undoubtedly influenced his acceptance of the plan to send the D.M.C. in a large sweeping movement to the east to take Beersheba from the desert flank. Both at Kimberley and Bloemfontein in South Africa, the same general plan had been used. An attack to feint to one side and a cavalry envelopment of the other flank. Allenby had participated in both Boer War battles which were complete successes against the Boer defenders.[11]

The plan to use mounted forces against Beersheba was predicated on the requirement for security in speed. Only the mounted forces had operational mobility to move the long distances in the desert quickly and thereby prevent inevitable detection in a landscape largely devoid of overhead concealment. Local air superiority substantially reduced observation flights by the Germans and prevented the Germans from determining the exact size and route of D.M.C. units on the move to Beersheba.

The D.M.C. began preparations for the battle as early as May 1917 when they surveyed and improved intermediate well sites. The Turks had destroyed many of the wells to prevent their use by the British forces. Although the wells could not supply but a small portion of the water required for the movement of the entire corps, they would be of some use during the operation and were put back into service by attached Royal Engineer units.[12]

By October 1917, the stage had been set and the logistical preparations made for the giant envelopment that would collapse the Gaza-Beersheba line. This maneuver would force the Turco-German forces back towards more defensible terrain around Jerusalem. Allenby ordered an aggressive mounted patrolling effort to condition the Turks and Germans to the presence of the D.M.C. units around Beersheba. Extensive patrolling assisted in the reinforcement of the deception plan. The deception story involved the mounted units of the D.M.C. making a demonstration at Beersheba while the real main attack would be against Gaza. By placing the D.M.C. mounted units on patrol around Beersheba, the deception plan would be reinforced and the D.M.C. would collect valuable information regarding the actual main attack.

The mission of the D.M.C. was to move to, and assail, the southern and eastern approaches to Beersheba. The corps would envelop the flank which was protected by the desert by capitalizing on its superior tactical and operational mobility.

The tactical mobility was provided by the horse mounted forces when in contact with the enemy. It allowed the Light Horse and cavalry to move expeditiously about the battlefield to engage the enemy at different points faster than infantry.

Operational mobility was also provided by the horse mounted forces as part of the corps. The entire corps was mounted and could, as one of the three corps of the E.E.F., conduct major movements out of contact with the enemy, but in support of the army.

The tactical objectives of Tel el Saba (also known as Tell es Sabe) and Tel el Sakati (also known as Bir es Sqati) to the northeast and east of town respectively, would provide the key terrain from which to overwatch the 20th Corps infantry and D.M.C. attack on Beersheba. Additionally, capture of Tel el Sakati would dominate the approaches from Hebron and prevent the Timely arrival of reserve troops to reinforce the Beersheba garrison.[13]

On the afternoon of 28 October 1917, the regiments of the D.M.C. began their march on Beersheba.[14] Moving largely at night, the corps prevented observation by the occasional enemy aircraft that managed to get across the front lines. The troopers and their horses were also able to conserve water by moving during the cooler portion of the day.

Some units were able to stop and water at the

intermediate well sites enroute. However, due to the strict timetable, and lack of enough water, the majority of horses and troopers got no water and had to rely solely on their quart canteens. By the evening of 30 October, many horses and soldiers had run out of water and had gone for 36-48 hours without any water resupply.[15]

On the evening of 30 October the regiments moved into their positions around Beersheba and remained hidden in the wadis to prevent detection. Chauvel established his command post on a hill several kilometers to the south of Beersheba where he had an uninterrupted view of the town and its approaches.[16]

Turkish troops garrisoning the town numbered approximately 4,400 and were of excellent quality, superior to the average Turkish soldier.[17] No indications are given in historical accounts as to why the town was garrisoned with Yilderim (Turkish 'storm troop' equivalent); however, it can be assumed that it was related to the importance of the wells in the town. Since no key facilities were located between Gaza and Beersheba, the decision to place the Yilderim in the town was most likely related to the relative worth of the wells.

It would be important to remember that even the regular Turkish soldiers were held in high regards for their martial abilities by the Allies. Enured to hardship and used to poor conditions, the Turkish soldiers were tough opponents. It is also important to remember that the Turks had established their military reputation early in the war when they defeated the Allied invasion of Gallipcli in 1915. They were not easily beaten.

Due to the lack of obstacle supplies, wire had not been strung all the way around the town and the defenses were incomplete or non-existant on the southern and southeastern approaches.[18] Aerial reconnaissance by the British and Australians confirmed the lack of obstacles in the Pastern portion of the defenses.

Because the town of Beersheba lies in a valley, observation from the town is limited to the near ridgelines. Ismet Bey depended upon aerial observation and artillery observers in the minaret of the mosque to alert the garrison as to the approach of enemy forces.[19] Weak Turkish cavalry units were unable to patrol far from their support and provided little information. The Turkish cavalry units were mounted on poorly conditioned horses. Lack of fodder and good horses placed the Turkish cavalry at a distinct disavantage. The total number of Turkish cavalry located in the area of operations never totaled more than 3,000. They were outnumbered by about 6.5:1. Qualitatively, the Turkish cavalry horses were no match for the better fed and cared for D.M.C. horses, many from Australia.

For these reasons the Turkish cavalry was never risked by its commanders and generally did not venture far from their lines. Because they were weak and remained near their own lines, the Turkish cavalry never posed a serious threat to the D.M.C. At Beersheba the Turkish cavalry manned pickets and conducted local patrols around the town.

While Chauvel had been given the order to capture the town in one day, a specific timeline had not been dictated to him. Cooperation with the 20th Corps attacking Beersheba on hiis flank was effected by the amicable relationship between Chauvel and his former commander, Chetwode. Both were responsible for attacking the town in a coordinated fashion. 20th Corps would begin the attack from the southwest and fix the enemy defenses. Once the Turks had drawn their reserves to the western side of the town, D.M.C. would attack the relatively open eastern flank and seize the town.[20]

Since the attack commenced at 0555 hours on 31 October, the D.M.C. theoretically had the entire day for the capture of the town. Realistically however, the town had to be seized no later than sundown or darkness would prevent further operations. Additionally, troop exhaustion and lack of water would force the withdrawal of the E.E.F. if Beersheba was not captured by dusk.

This gave Chauvel about eleven hours of daylight to

execute his plan.[21]

Dispositions for the D.M.C. attack were made with two of the three divisions conducting attacks adjacent to the 20th Corps and the third in reserve. ANZAC Mounted Division was given the task to seize the road and dominating hills on the northeastern and eastern sides of the town. The Yeomanry Mounted Division would tie-in with the 20th Corps cavalry which was screening their own corps' right flank. The Australian Mounted Division (3rd and 4th Light Horse Brigades and 5th Cavalry Brigade) was in reserve between, and to the rear, of the other two D.M.C. divisions.[22]

Tel el Sakati was stormed by the New Zealanders of ANZAC Mounted Division and captured at about 1300 hours after a vicious assault and hand-to-hand combat. This gave control of the approaches from Jerusalem and Hebron to the D.M.C. At 1500 hours a dismounted attack captured the Tel el Saba opening a major avenue into Beersheba. Both fights were hard uphill battles and exhausted the ANZAC units which had to attack during the heat of the day.[23]

Of importance was the fact that both artillery and machine guns were driven from the Tel el Saba and Tel el Sakati positions. This prevented enfilading fires on the approaches to Beersheba along the roads from both the east and the plain in the south. The potential for major damage to a

D.M.C. attack was negated and the way opened for an advance from the southeast and south.

20th Corps attacked into some of the strongest parts of the prepared defensive works and made slow headway as a result. Although the attacking forces were larger, the advantages to the defenders allowed the Turks to prevent major gains by the attacking infantry.

As the day wore on, Chauvel became acutely aware of the problem that faced not only his corps but the entire E.E.F. Failure to capture the wells would not just lose the battle but delay the entire campaign. Failure to seize the wells would force the withdrawal of the D.M.C. and the 20th Corps south to the wells towards the coast. Few options were remaining when Chauvel called for the commanders of the Yeomanry and Australian Divisions to meet with him.[24]

Briefing the situation to his subordinates, Chauvel then asked for their opinions. What faced the D.M.C. was a time consuming and difficult dismounted advance across several kilometers of open ground. The advance would be covered by machine guns and field artillery and would have to be accomplished before sundown at 1650 hours. The situation was a classic military problem. A difficult mission, limited time, and a prospect for severe defeat should they fail. The time was 1600 hours.

The Australian brigadier commanding the 4th Light Horse Brigade, Brigadier Grant, stepped forward and stated that he could seize the town. He requested permission to conduct his action with a "free hand." Chauvel probably responded more out of curiosity when he asked Grant what plan he would use. Grant's answer is one of the great responses of modern warfare when he stated "A cavalry attack, sir."[25] Within the context of the situation it was quite incredible that a mounted infantry force would propose to conduct a "cavalry attack," something which fell outside of Light Horse doctrine. It had never been done before by the Light Horse.

Brigadier P. D. Fitzgerald of the Yeomanry Division immediately registered disagreement and requested that his troops be allowed to conduct the attack since they were armed with swords. Chauvel weighed the choices, to allow Light Horse, mounted infantry, to charge immediately, or, wait and allow the Yeomanry unit to move forward and charge. The Yeomanry were several kilometers further south than the 4th Light Horse Brigade. It would take longer for them to reach the start line.

The risks involved were the possible loss of daylight and the fact the Light Horse was not equipped to close with the enemy in a traditional charge by shock action. The possibility that daylight would fade before the Yeomanry could be committed to action was a real consideration.

The 4th Light Horse Brigade was located much closer to Beersheba and could be in action in a much shorter time. Chauvel turned back to General Hodgson, commander of the Australian Mounted Division, and ordered, "Put Grant straight at it."[26] This set into motion the single most important charge by an Allied mounted force during the war. It was the beginning of a chain of events which emphasized both tactical and operational mobility on the battlefields of the Eastern Theater.

Grant alerted the closest of two regiments, the 4th and 12th Light Horse Regiments and by 1630 hours they were forming on their initial start lines. With about twenty minutes of daylight left, the regiments began movement toward Beersheba first at the walk, then at the trot.

The squadrons of each regiment were formed in "line extended." Successive squadrons trailed in line. The regiments would have had a frontage of three troops, about 100 men. The 1910 Light Horse Manual does not show such a formation for either regimental or brigade drill. This was a typical cavalry formation never used in combat before by the Light Horse.[27]

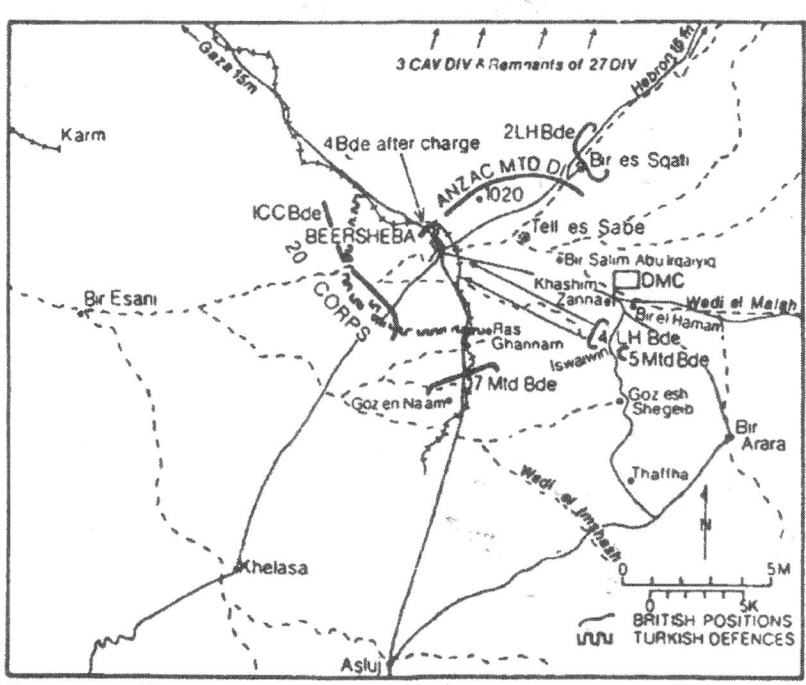

The capture of Beersheba, 31 October 1917

As the squadrons of the 4th Regiment moved out, the 12th aligned itself and formed on the left flank of the 4th. With a brigade front of two squadrons and the others in trail, the brigade had a frontage of about two hundred men with the remainder in depth. The troopers of the brigade immediately opened their intervals to about five yards to prevent mass casualties from artillery or machinegun fire. At a distance of about two and a half kilometers from Turkish trenches the regiments broke into a full gallop and closed on the enemy's positions.

Trained as they had been in Eygpt by "Dad" Forsyth in 1915, the troopers drew their seventeen inch Enfield bayonets and brandished them as they would swords above their heads. Counting on the Australians to dismount and attack on foot, the Turkish gunners set their sights to 1,600 meters. As the charge gained momentum and speed, the Turks lost their composure and forgot to adjust the sights on their weapons.[28] Within a very short time the Australians had passed "under the guns" and the Turkish rounds were flying over their heads. The trajectory of the Turkish guns allowed the Light Horsemen to close to within a few meters of the defensive positions before the shortened line of sight and trajectory were coincidental and were able to cause further casualties.

The first line of squadrons in the regiments jumped the trenches and galloped to the Turkish bivouac area before dismounting and fighting back by first clearing the reserve and support trenches. The second line of squadrons jumped the main line of trenches, dismounted and immediately began clearing in a sharp bayonet engagement. The third squadron uismounted in front of the main trenches and supported the attack of the second on the main trenches.[29]

The battle was rough and tumble, hand-to-hand but also very short. The majority of the deaths on the Turkish side were from the point of the bayonet.[30] The 12th Light Horse Regiment avoided a number of the intermittent trenches and rushed into the town. Demolition of the wells by the Germans was prevented by the audacity of the charge which completely caught the defenders within the town off guard. By nightfall the remaining defenders had surrendered or fled to the north with their commander, Ismet Bey.

The D.M.C. placed a screen line around the town but did not pursue, a point of contention later between the Imperial Staff and Allenby.[31] Allenby stuck by his subordinate, Chauvel, and argued the point that pursuit would have been impossible under the circumstances of troop exhaustion and lack of water.

While the pursuit of the defeated Turks would have been desirable, it had never been within the scope of the operation. The collapse of the Gaza Beersheba line was contingent upon the fall of Beersheba, not the complete destruction of the Turkish forces in the area. The destruction of the Turkish forces could afford to wait since no other point between Gaza and Beersheba offered such a key and decisive point as Beersheba.

The Turks were forced to fall back on their lines in order to reconstitute a new defensive line.

The immediate results of the battle were a tremendous moral victory for the E.E.F. which had failed to break the Gaza line twice that year. Amazingly, the cost was relatively small considering the action which occurred. Only thirty one men had been killed and thirty six wounded in a charge against dug in infantry, machine guns, and howitzers. Seventy horses died.[32] The Turkish dead were never counted but over 3,000 Turks were taken prisoner.

The wells were seized largely intact allowing for the movement of the E.E.F. away from the coast and into central Judea. The fall of Beersheba destroyed the continuity of the Turco-German defense. It forced the Turks and Germans to find a new natural line of defense based on the terrain further north.

The charge at Beersheba demonstrated the audacity of the Australian commanders. The contrast between their actions and that of the Yeomanry again emphasizes the basic differences between the two. Grant did not have to be prompted to make the recommendation to Chauvel that his brigade charge. The Yeomanry commander only stepped forward after the Australians had proposed that Light Horse be used to conduct a cavalry action. Grant's suggestion demonstrated not only initiative for his timely remark but tremendous flexibility for recommending a non-traditional solution.

On the lesser side, the action at Beersheba established mounted charges as an effective tactical solution again. On a larger scale, the battle reinforced the use of the mounted forces for operational maneuver. The D.M.C. proved its worth as a mounted, corps maneuver force by its rapid move around the flank of the Turkish defenses. This operation was carried out as a separate major operation whereby the other two corps fixed the enemy to the front while the D.M.C. moved around an exposed flank. The operational use of the corps is overshadowed by the successful tactical use of the mounted forces in the charge at Beersheba. It is no less important.

As a final result, the action at Beersheba marked the beginning point in the training, equipping, and the employment of the majority of Light Horse units from mounted infantry to cavalry units.

Results of the Charge at Beersheba

> Quite apart from the vital part they had played in the capture of Beersheba, the charge of the 4th Australian Light Horse Brigade set the standard for the rest of the campaign. It had shown that under certain circumstances cavalry might still be used for shock action, and it inspired a spirit of dash and daring which the rest of Allenby's cavalry was quick to emulate.[33]

The successful charge of the Australians at Beersheba had an amazing effect of the mounted forces of the E.E.F. Word spread quickly, as it might be imagined, that not only had there been a successful charge of mounted forces against an entrenched enemy, but the scale of the charge and the results it wrought were of major significance. The fact the charge occurred at what appeared to be the critical point in the battle encouraged embellishment of the lore. What the Australians did was exceptional based strictly on the fact that they were mounted infantry.

The charge at Beersheba was the largest horse mounted charge of Western cavalry forces during the First World War. The charge of a brigade of three regiments with supporting arms was never matched in other theaters by the size, nor by its significance. Smaller, regimental sized charges took place in Western Europe during the closing days of the war but did not have the importance on battles or campaigns that the charge at Beersheba did.

The 4th Australian Light Horse Brigade charge collapsed the continuity of the Turkish defense along the entire front in a single action conducted at a critical point in the battle. Tactically, it was an example of the bold use of mounted forces in order to influence the action at a decisive point. It set a tremendous precedence for the other horse mounted forces of the E.E.F. which lost no time attempting their own charges. The success both tactically and operationally at Beersheba established the basis for the plan for Megiddo by Allenby.

Other factors certainly combined with the charge of the 4th Light Horse Brigade to change the tactical employment and armament of the Australian Mounted Division. The circumstances for the charge at Beersheba was only the beginning of a situation in the Eastern Theater which saw the deterioration of the Turco-German forces. There were always much less well supplied than corresponding units fighting on the Western Front for Germany. They had less artillery, aircraft, and machine guns than supplied to the same sized units on the Western Front. After the battle at Romani in July 1916, when the Turco-German forces went on the defensive for the remainder of the war, the supply of important defensive materiel such as barbed wire began to dwindle.

The lack of a key element of obstacle materiel, barbed wire, proved to be decisive not only at Beersheba but for the battles which followed. Without barbed wire, there was little to stop the horse mounted units from closing quickly on defensive positions when the terrain allowed. This mobility allowed for the success of the mounted units of the E.E.F.

The charge at Beersheba set off a series of cavalry actions not seen before in the Eastern Theater or the Western Front. In very short order the Yeomanry conducted a three squadron charge at Huj on 8 November 1917, and two regiments charged at El Mughar Ridge, 13 November 1917.

Two regiments of New Zealand Mounted Rifles charged at Ayun Kara, 14 November 1917. All charges were successful and netted a large number of prisoners and captured materiel. The charge at Huj and El Mughar resulted in large numbers of enemy killed.

These actions were noteworthy in respect to the enemy forces they faced. At Huj alone, the Yeomanry faced a rearguard force of 2,000 Turkish infantrymen, two field artillery batteries, a mountain gun battery, and a company of machine guns. Three composite squadrons charged, about three hundred fifty cavalrymen. The other actions were similar in respect to the numbers involved. In no case were the mounted soldiers superior in numbers to the enemy they faced.

The numbers speak for themselves when the effects of Beersheba are measured quantitatively. Before Beersheba, only one charge had been conducted by the British in the Middle East. Although it was successful, it was also against Arab tribesmen who were not extremely well armed, trained, or in prepared positions. Other charges had occurred by the Light Horse at Katia and Magdhaba, none by the Yeomanry until after Beersheba. Katia failed due to the terrain and those at Magdhaba were accidental actions, a result of sheer impulse at the last minute, never classified as a true cavalry charge but mounted attacks. After Beersheba however, in the last twelve months of the war, upwards of thirty charges occurred of at least squadron size or greater, at least two involving two regiments.

The Yeomanry, which had had problems adapting to tactical modifications brought about by the Boer War, requiring for the increased reliance on the rifle and dismounted action, reverted completely to mounted action again. Interestingly, the Yeomanry never quite transitioned to their role as specified in doctrine and were quick to revert to a totally mounted role. While dismounting to fight with the rifle had proven successful, it was difficult for the Yeomanry to break old habits.

The success of the Australian 4th Light Horse Brigade at Beersheba had a similar effect on the Australians and their tactics. Like the Yeomanry, once it was demonstrated that mounted action could succeed, the Australians began practicing the technique themselves. Commanders of some Light Horse units began practicing sword drill with bayonets. However, due to the circumstances the Australians continued to fight a number of engagements as mounted infantry throughout the next six months. Primarily employed in the Jordan Valley throughout the spring and summer, they did not experience another chance to charge as cavalry.

Cavalrymen throughout the E.E.F. felt vindicated. A charge the scope of which had not been possible since 1914 on the Western front had occurred in a major battle under circumstances thought to be disadvantageous to mounted action. A charge across a wide expanse of open ground against entrenched enemy infantry, machine guns, and field artillery was thought to be impossible without suffering disastrous losses. What was even more incredible was that the charge was conducted by Light Horsemen mounted infantry.

This was the type of war that cavalrymen had been waiting for during three years of war when barbed wire, entrenchments, and the machine gun were thought to have negated the effects of the charge. The actual effect on the mounted forces of the E.E.F. were almost immediate.

Cavalrymen whose doctrine taught them to fight as dismounted infantry quickly reevaluated their mission to provide shock action and tactical mobility. While it was hard to break old traditions such as the mounted charge, the officers and men of the Yeomanry had gradually become more adept at riding to the battle and fighting according to the pre-war doctrine which required the primary weapon to be the rifle. At the battles for Gaza the Yeomanry began executing the doctrine of riding to the battle site and dismounting to fight. The action at Beersheba reversed this trend and caused them to consider anew the use of the sword.

Cavalrymen who heard of the charge at Beersheba must

have felt a certain sense of disappointment. The charge was conducted by mounted infantrymen, not cavalry, even though cavalry was present on the battlefield. This was not the doctrinal use of the mounted infantry and it was felt for some time afterwards by British cavalrymen that the cavalry should have been given the chance to charge.

The success of a cavalry charge against dug in infantry might not have been as successful as the cavalrymen thought. One major reason militated against such success. The cavalry was armed to charge with the sword. The success at Beersheba was a result of the Light Horse being able to dismount and rout the Turks out of the trenches with the bayonet, a task for which the Yeomanry would have been hard pressed to accomplish due to their cavalry training and mounted orientation.

While the cavalry might have felt regret at not having been the ones to conduct the charge, they also probably felt a natural exhilaration that the place of the horse had been returned to a war characterized by increasing firepower and static positioning on the battlefields of Europe. For the horse mounted forces in the Mid-East, the biggest chance was yet to come.

NOTES

1. Edmund Dane, <u>British Campaigns in the Near East, 1914-1918, Vol. II</u> (London: Hodder and Stoughton,

1919, p. 90.

2. Sir Archibald Murray, Sir Archibald Murray's Despatches, (London: J. M. Dent and Sons, Ltd., 1920), p. 165; Hill, Chauvel of the Light Horse, p. 108.

3. Hill, Chauvel of the Light Horse, pp. 119-120.

4. Firkins, The Australians in Nine Wars, p. 79.

5. Jones, The Australian Light Horse, p. 89.

6. FM 100-5, Operations (Headquarters, Department of the Army, 5 May 1986), p. 10. Operational art is defined as "...the employment of military forces to attain strategic goals through ...major operations." "A major operation comprises the coordinated actions of large forces (in this case a mounted corps acting semi-independently) in a single phase of a campaign or in a critical battle (3d Gaza/Beersheba). Major operations decide the course of campaigns." In retrospect, the capture of Beersheba was clearly a major operation by a corps sized element which decided the course of the remainder of the campaign in the Middle East. The battle for Beersheba crosses the boundaries of a tactical action at the regimental and divisional level into the sphere of operational art at the corps level according to current U.S. doctrinal definitions.

7. Based upon author's visit to the Beersheba battle site in February, 1981 during a field training exercise.

8. Mark Cocker, Richard Meinertzhagen: Soldier,

Scientist and Spy (London: Secker and Warburg, 1989), p. 103.

    9. Ibid.

    10. Hill, Chauvel of the Light Horse, p. 109.

    11. Bullock, Allenby's War: The Palestine-Arabian Campaigns 1916-1918, pp. 79-80, 83; Hill, Chauvel of the Light Horse, p. 21.

    12. Major H. 0. Locke With the British Army in the Holy Land (London: Robert Scott Roxburghe House, 1919), p. 52.

    13. John Ellis, Cavalry (New York: G. P. Putnam's Sons, 1978), pp. 56-57.

    14. Jones, The Australian Light Horse, p. 93.

    15. Ibid., pp. 96-97.

    16. Lunt, Charge to Glory, p. 197; Hill, Chauvel of the Light Horse, p. 133.

    17. Bullock, Allenby's War: The Palestine-Arabian Campaigns 1916-1918, p. 73.

    18. Lieutenant-Colonel Prioux, translated by Captain W. B. Bradford, "Course in Cavalry," lecture presented to the French Army War College, Encole Superieure de Guerre, 1923-1924, p. 344.

    19. The Light Horsemen, produced by Simon Wincer and directed by Ian Jones, 106 min., RKO Pictures,

1988, videocassette.

20. Cyril Falls, <u>Military Operations Egypt and Palestine From June 1917 to the End of the War, Part II</u> (London: His

Majesty's Stationery Office, 1930), pp. 686-688; Hill, <u>Ctauvel of the Light Horse,</u> p. 20.

21. Time factors are computed from the following sources which cite dawn and dusk times: Wavell, <u>The Palestine Campaigns, p.72</u>; Gullett, <u>The Australian Imperial Force in Sinai and Palestine, 1914-1918,</u> p. 386.

22. Gullett, <u>The Australian Imperial Force in Sinai and Palestine,</u> Map 15.

23. Ibid., pp. 388-391. The horse mounted units attacked mounted, dismounted under cover and assaulted dismounted. Few casualties were taken during mounted movement but increased.

24. Laffin, <u>ANZACS at War,</u> p. 81; Jones, <u>The Australian Light Horse,</u> pp. 97-98.

25. Hill, <u>Chauvel of the Light Horse,</u> p. 98.

26. Ibid., p. 98.

27. Warner, <u>The British Cavalry,</u> p. 183.

28. Bullock, <u>Allenby's War: The Palestine-Arabian Campaigns 1916-1918,</u> p. 56.

29. Jones, <u>The Australian Light Horse,</u> pp. 102-

104.
30. Lunt, Charge to Glory, p. 200.

31. Hill, Chauvel of the Light Horse, p. 137.

32. Ibid., p. 128.

33. "Cavalry Operations During World War," Fort Riley, KS, The Cavalry School, 1929, No. 24, p. 10; "The Palestine Campaign," Fort Riley, KS, The Cavalry School, 1922-1923, pp. 190-192.

CHAPTER 4 - FROM MOUNTED INFANTRY TO CAVALRY

Transition Between the Battles

> In order to demonstrate that mounted attack on infantry is never possible, it would be necessary to prove that infantry is never of poor quality, never demoralized by disaster, never out of ammunition, never in a position where a sudden attack without warning at short range is possible, due to abundant cover, fog, rain, etc. It would also be necessary to demonstrate that panic even among good troops, is no longer an element to be reckoned with and it is also necessary to ignore the fact that modern cavalry or mounted infantry at the end of a charge, having reached a desirable position, can jump off their horses and fight on foot.
> Brigadier General James Parker U.S. Army,
> The Mounted Rifleman (1916)[1]

During the course of the year between October 1917 and October 1918, the Light Horse units were largely engaged in the exploitation of the withdrawing Turkish and German forces. The E.E.F. managed to cover about twice the distance in this last year of the war than they had covered in the preceeding two years.

Between the action at Beersheba until the last battle at

Megiddo, the Australian Light Horse units changed their general tactical methods of operation based upon the situation confronting them. After the battle at Beersheba, the Turks and Germans conducted a series of delays as their retreating forces sought defensible terrain. Turkish soldiers were weakened because of a lack of organized resupply and because many of their better leaders were killed. The Light Horse units took advantage of the weakened enemy situation by conducting cavalry type missions.

The difference in the employment of the mounted forces in the Battle of Megiddo was the result of a year long transition beginning with the battle at Beersheba in October 1917. The resulting charge, a tactical employment, was purely chance, driven by the expediency of the moment. The success on the tactical level however, led to increased emphasis on the use of the mounted arms at the operational level.

The charge at Beersheba emboldened the Australians to conduct more mounted operations. This, combined with their duties in the Jordan Valley during the summer of 1918 in a security role, forced them more to a cavalry employment than mounted infantry. In roles more traditionally linked to cavalry, the Light Horse units conducted raids, mounted patrols, and performed an economy of force mission on the right flank of the E.E.F.

The disintegration of the Turkish armies due to combat attrition and other causes changed the complexion of the battlefield. Fewer troops were available for the Turks to form integrated defensive lines. Additionally, the distances that had to be defended in northern Palestine had increased greatly from the distances in the Sinai and Negev. The desert no longer provided an unassailable flank since water was more plentiful. Both sides could move further away from the Mediterranean coast.

These conditions of fewer troops to defend a contiguous line and greater expanses of terrain to defend were disadvantages to the Turks and Germans. Gaps in the Turkish lines could be penetrated and exploited by mounted elements more readily. The mounted elements of the D.M.C. were able to cover the wide areas of their own lines in an effective manner. This forced the Australian Light Horse into cavalry economy of force missions.

By the time of the Battle of Megiddo in September 1918, some Light Horse units had experienced changes in tactical employment and in the armament of the regiments as well. In August 1918, the Australian Mounted Division issued swords to supplement its rifles and bayonets.[2] This significant change in weaponry signaled a change in basic tactical employment. Instead of the horse acting as a means of transportation to the battlefield, the horse became the means of transportation on the battlefield.

Major-General Hodgson initiated the move to obtain swords for the men of the Australian Mounted Division. Hodgson was a British regular cavalryman and was held in esteem by his Australian subordinates despite the fact all three brigades of his division were composed of, and commanded by, Australians. His request for swords was echoed by all the brigade commanders, especially the 4th Brigade which had charged at Beersheba under Brigadier Grant with drawn bayonets.[3]

Major-General E. W. C. Chaytor, commander of the ANZAC Mounted Division, deferred arming his units with the sword. Despite successes of the Indian cavalry units fighting in the Jordan Valley along side Chaytor's force, Chaytor decided to employ his division as mounted infantry.[4]

The majority of the Light Horse however, was rearmed as cavalry by September 1918 in time for the last major offensive. The significance of this act demonstrates a major turn in the philosophy of the Light Horse commanders who rearmed with the Pattern 1908 British cavalry sword. The sword is an entirely offensive weapon. It has no real utility in the defense, and the straight bladed sword, as used by the British and Australians, was meant to be used strictly in charges.

The Pattern 1908 sword is a thrusting weapon. Its blade is extremely narrow and has no cutting surfaces along its edges. The point is meant to be the offensive part of the weapon and it is only of value when the cavalryman using it is moving forward towards the enemy. Unlike the curved saber, which can be used while a soldier is not moving due to the ability to slash with the blade, the sword cannot be used to perform a dual role. While the sword may be used to parry the thrust of other edged weapons, the blade does not allow for the edges to be used as cutting surfaces as does the saber. In order to use the sword, the point must be thrust into the opponent. The most effective way to use the sword is in consonance with some form of forward momentum. The horse provided this momentum.

General Chauvel did not miss the chance for his horse mounted units to influence the outcome of the entire campaign. He acquiesed to the decision to arm the Australian Mounted Division with swords which meant that all the Australians under his command for the Megiddo battle would be armed as cavalry. In total, he would have the 4th Cavalry Division, 5th Cavalry Division, and the Australian Mounted Division, a complete cavalry corps in the truest sense.

Against the increasingly demoralized Turkish soldiers a sword charge and its attending shock action proved to be successful in several instances after Beersheba. Since the Turkish forces were in retreat, the sword proved to be the ideal weapon for the exploitation and pursuit.

The Battle of Megiddo

Megiddo and Armageddon are the same place and same series of engagements. Megiddo is the name given to the ancient city located on a key hill leading into the Valley of Jezreel and Armageddon is the Anglicization of the Hebrew words meaning "Mount Megiddo."[5]

The battle of Megiddo was important for several reasons. It became a hallmark example of mobile warfare in the First World War because of its short duration, the large cavalry forces involved, and the dramatic results. Megiddo exemplified on a much larger level what had been started by the Australians at Beersheba, the return of tactical and operational mobility to the battlefield.

The Meggido battle was designed to quickly and completely eliminate Turkey from the war.[6] The general plan called for the use of infantry forces to penetrate the Turkish defenses. The D.M.C. would exploit the breach by turning the Turkish right flank and envelop the Turkish VII and VIII Armies. The execution of the plan was so successful that the war ended five weeks after the initial penetration. The exploitation and pursuit of Turkish forces never allowed a major defense to be mounted. After the initial penetration of Turkish lines, the war was fought almost entirely by the Commonwealth horse mounted forces.

Megiddo quickly turned into a massive exploitation and pursuit. The battle led to the final defeat of the Turkish and German forces in Palestine and Syria. It contains both tactical and operational mounted maneuver on a scale not previously experienced in the Middle-East or on the Western Front.[7] Tactical maneuver was demonstrated because of the large number of charges and operational maneuver because of the depth and size of the penetration by the D.M.C.

The battle began on 19 September 1918 and was the culmination of intensive deception and logistical preparations over the preceding nine months. Allenby's forces consolidated their positions from a line extending roughly north of Jaffa to the Dead Sea in the Jordan Valley. The Battle of Megiddo stretched from the Mediterreanean coast to the Jordan Valley with the primary engagements occurring along the coastal area (the Plain of Sharon) and in the central hills of Samaria. The trace of opposing forces prior to the battle was about 80 kilometers if curves and turns in the line are measured.[8]

The general situation existing on the eve of the last major battle fought in Palestine during the First World War found three Turkish Armies opposing the E.E.F. Two of the armies, the VII and VIII Armies, were arrayed from the Mediterranean to the Jordan River. The Turkish IV Army ran from the Jordan River east toward Amman and covered the flank approach from the desert. Troops in the fighting line west of the Jordan River numbered approximately 35,000 Turks and Germans to about 69,000 Commonwealth forces. The ratio of fighting strength was about 2:1 on the west side of the Jordan River.[9]

After the fall of Jerusalem to the E.E.F. in December 1917, the line of opposing troops moved north a relatively short distance. This line, described previously, was approximately forty kilometers north of Jerusalem. Allenby might have kept pushing the Turkish armies further back had events in Europe not affected his campaign. Seasoned troops had to be stripped from the E.E.F. during the March 1918 German Western Front offensive in order to reinforce the Allies in Europe. This unplanned reduction of forces caused Allenby to halt his offensive to the north until the troop strength could be built up again.[10]

Units shipped to France included a number of infantry battalions and the majority of the Yeomanry regiments. The troops were rushed to the battlefields on the Western Front to stem the advance of the German armies. Ironically, the troops that were becoming some of the most valuable to Allenby (especially after Beersheba), the Yeomanry, were sent as reorganized machine gun battalions.

The Australian Light Horse Regiments remained in the theater and two, the 14th and 15th Regiments, were reorganized into the 5th Light Horse Brigade having formerly been camel mounted. The Light Horse units at this time formed only about 40% of the "cavalry" strength of the E.E.F. They were able to maintain their relative strength in the mounted corps by the addition of the 14th and 15th Regiments as the 5th Light Horse Brigade. Overall, the Light Horse and New Zealanders composed over half of all horse mounted forces in the E.E.F.

Other than divisional cavalry squadrons, all horse mounted units of the E.E.F. came under the command of Lieutenant-General Chauvel of the Desert Mounted Corps and formed the largest tactical cavalry force in western history under a single commander. His corps eventually had over 28,000 horsemen in it.[11]

The departure of seasoned units from the E.E.F. for France coincided with the planned arrival of a number of troops from the Indian Army. Originally scheduled to move to the Eastern Theater to supplement Allenby's forces, the Indian Army troops arrived in time to replace the large numbers enroute to the Western Front.

While the majority of troops under Allenby remained

infantry, another division of cavalry was added to the army organization. The significance of the addition of another cavalry division was obviously a result of the major successes achieved not only at Beersheba but during the subsequent operations along the Philistine Plain in the drive north from Gaza to Jerusalem. Had the Yeomanry mounted division not been removed, it is possible that another cavalry corps would have been formed.

The influx of cavalry units signaled the importance of horse mounted units on the battlefield again. Cavalry corps had not been employed in Europe since the beginning days of WWI. The formation of one active corps was significant, two would have been of major significance since they had essentially disappeared from the European setting.

The relative fighting strength of the infantry in Allenby's army was reduced despite the addition of the Indian Army infantry battalions. These battalions had come from garrisons in India or the Salonika and Macedonian fronts. Comparatively inexperienced except in limited trench warfare, they had only a few weeks to become proficient in offensive tactics. In terms of combat power, the new replacement battalions did not compare favorably to those removed. Consequently, the burden on the Light Horse in particular, and of cavalry in general, increased. Reliance on the mounted forces for economy of force missions kept the D.M.C. units constantly employed filling the gaps for the experienced, departing infantry.

In order to maintain some semblance of offensive action, Allenby sought to cut the rail line from Damascus to Amman. Because the E.E.F. was reorganizing due to the loss of units to Europe, Allenby could not conduct major operations. It was decided that a large scale raid would keep the Turks on the defensive and help maintain the morale of the E.E.F. forces in the Jordan Valley. A large raid by the D.M.C. on the eastern side of the Jordan River in May 1918 failed and the opposing force positions remained largely static until the battle of Megiddo began.

During the time following the Amman raid until the battle at Megiddo, Allenby deployed his units according to an elaborate deception plan to make the Turks think that he was going to attack with his mounted corps on the exposed desert flank to the east of the Jordan Valley. Allenby maintained a force named after its commander, Major-General Chaytor, in the Jordan Valley to demonstrate in front of the Turks and portray a major effort. Chaytor's task was to deceive the Turks into thinking that the D.M.C. was being marshaled there. The use of the D.M.C. supported the deception plan since the D.M.C. had normally led all major offensive actions.

Chaytor's Force was an ad hoc grouping of forces which conducted an economy of force and deception effort on the extreme right flank of the E.E.F.[12] Mounted units of Chaytor's Force made a number of demonstrations to encourage the Turks and Germans to believe that the main portion of the mounted forces were still in the Jordan Valley.

Chaytor used the cavalry and Light Horse in his sector to demonstrate the presence of mounted forces. Turkish and German intelligence was led to believe that the presence of the mounted arms in the area of the Jordan indicated the future main effort of the army based upon established precedence.[13] The Turco-German command was successfully deceived as to the actual location of the main attack along the Mediterranean coast. A sizable number of Turkish troops were concentrated on the eastern side of the Jordan valley, well away from the main attack.

Several Light Horse regiments were detached from the D.M.C. and attached to the ANZAC Mounted Division to add credibility to Chaytor's demonstration. In the meantime, the reorganized D.M.C. moved to the extreme western end of the line and hid well away from the line of contact.[14] This movement happened gradually over a period of three months in order to maintain operational security. When the battle began in September 1918, the bulk of the E.E.F. was concentrated toward the Mediterranean coast. The eastern end of Allenby's line consisted of an economy of force effort in order to portray a main effort.

With the ANZAC Mounted Division detached, the three division D.M.C. prepared for the exploitation and pursuit of the Turco-German forces along the coastal plains and the central highlands. General Allenby, himself a cavalryman, had been instrumental in the development of such a plan calling for the operational maneuver of his mounted corps into the rear of the opposing armies.[15]

Allenby's experiences as a cavalry division commander in the early days of the war on the Western Front were certainly not tainted by the failure of the cavalry to maintain their mobility. The circumstances were now completely different and his successful use of the mounted corps at Beersheba in an operational maneuver to envelop the Turkish flank played a major factor in his continued use of the horse mounted arms.

Megiddo: Finding the 'G' in Gap

In the twelve days from the 19th to the 30th of September inclusive, the three cavalry divisions had marched over 200 miles, fought a number of minor actions, and captured more than 60,000 prisoners, 140 guns, and 500 machine guns.[16]

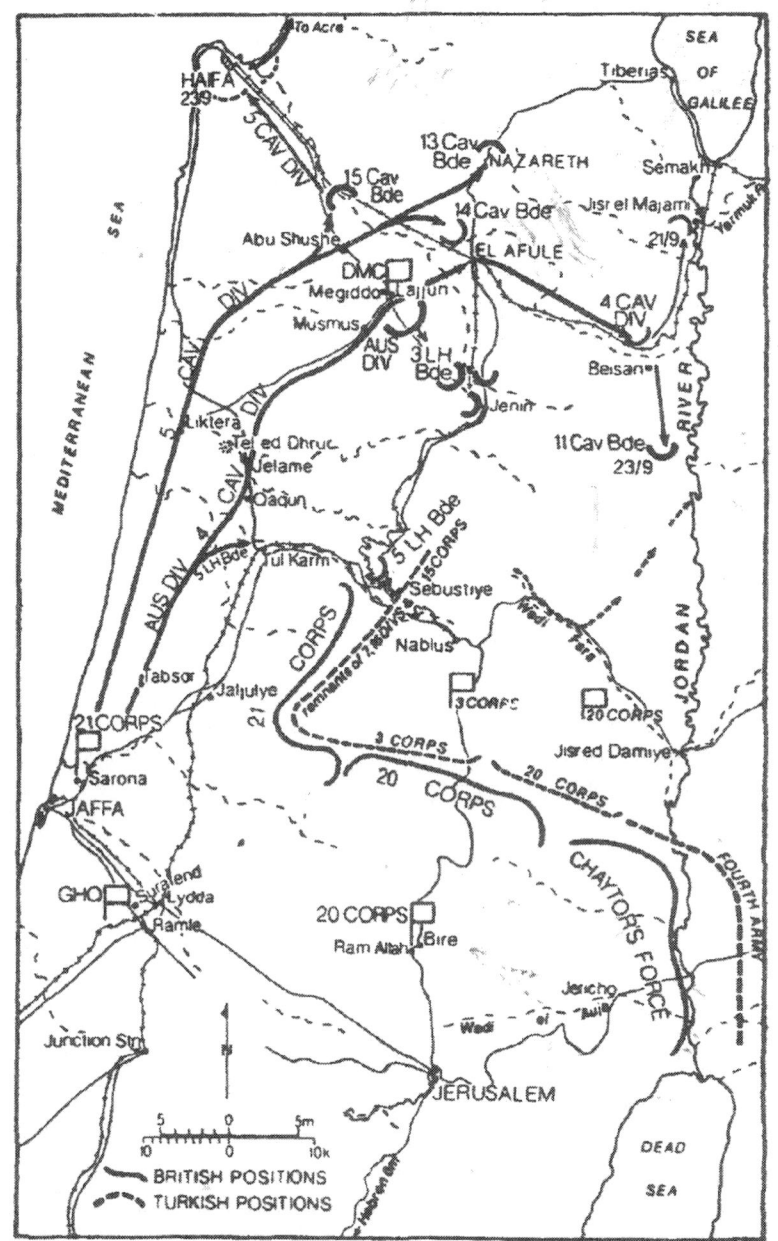

The destruction of Army Group F, 19-20 September 1918, and the development of Desert Mounted Corps operations to 23 September

The intervening engagements throughout 1918 changed the Australians' outlook on the tactical use of the Light Horse as cavalry instead of mounted infantry. Certainly Chauvel willingly sanctioned this change. His sanction of the Australian Mounted Division's arming with swords is an indication of his acceptance of the changing role of the Light Horsemen.

The changes in the missions of the Light Horse from mounted infantry to cavalry led to the difference in their employment at the Battle of Megiddo. Unlike the battle at Beersheba, Chauvel did not assign his Light Horse division, the Australian Mounted, an infantry objective or role. Instead, the unit was treated as a cavalry unit (as it was now equipped). Not even the rifle equipped British cavalry units were assigned dismounted tasks. Chauvel aptly demonstrated his ability to adapt to the new circumstances.

After the initial breakthrough on the 19th of September by the infantry, the Desert Mounted Corps quickly penetrated into the rear defensive zones. The initial penetration of the main defensive belt was conducted by the infantry divisions who opened a gap approximately twelve kilometers wide by ten kilometers deep. The D.M.C. attacked mounted in column through the gap formed by the infantry divisions and then deployed throughout northern and central Palestine. The order of march was the 5th Cavalry, 4th Cavalry, and Australian

Mounted Divisions.

No later than three hours after the initial artillery bombardment had begun, regiments of the 5th Cavalry were formed behind the advancing infantry in the breach. In the early morning hours the infantry had secured sufficient gains in the tactical depth of the Turkish defenses to insure that the reserve trenches could not interfere with the operation. The cavalry forces were free to begin their movements into the enemy rear.

Some resentment was felt by the Australian Mounted Division whose regiments had led every advance from Romani to Jerusalem. The Australian Mounted Division had no particular desire to follow the "Indian Cavalry" (4th and 5th Cavalry Divisions) in the line of march as a matter of pride.[17]

Immediately after the breakthrough along the coast, the divisions of the D.M.C. began their advance. The Australian Mounted Division, trailing the other cavalry divisions, was almost immediately ordered to turn from its advance to the northeast in order to take advantage of an opportunity to turn the Turkish flank. General Chauvel had the Australian Mounted move east and southeast to envelop retreating enemy forces attempting to escape the 20th Corps (British) located to the right rear of the Desert Mounted Corps. Moving east (perpendicular) to the difficult cross compartmentation which hindered lateral traffic ability for defenders and attackers, the

Australian Mounted Division began a series of movements to cut the lines of retreat for elements of the Turkish VII and VIII Armies.

This turning movement and reorientation of the Australian Mounted Division afforded them more flexibility in their actions. No longer tied to units on their flanks, the Australian Mounted Division began an advance by turning east through Samaria to Nablus and paralleling the Turco-German forces front lines. Nablus was well within the adjacent 20th Corps zone of action and was a significant communications hub with improved roads running north-south and northwest to southeast through central Samaria.18

Because the Australians were planning to fight mounted, armed with swords, it was very important that their speed provide them operational security and tactical shock action in their movements. Fighting in either the close hills of central Samaria, or in the towns, could have proven difficult for the new cavalry regiments of the Light Horse whose new weapon depended solely upon the tactical mobility of the horse. By taking advantage of the speed of movement and the disorientation of the Turkish and German defenders, the Australians would be able to close on the rear elements of the enemy forces before a viable defense could be established. It was in this regard that the Australians proved to be successful.

In less than twenty four hours after the start of the battle, the Light Horse regiments of the Australian Mounted Division had secured the right flank of .he corps. They had seized several important towns to include Tul Karm, Jenin, and Nablus in the process and cut the major lines of retreat through central Palestine. They were arrayed with the 5th Light Horse Brigade in the south, the 3rd Brigade in the north and the 4th Brigade supporting in the center, moving north to a position behind the 3rd Brigade.[19]

The main line of communication running north-south through central Palestine was seized along about a 20 kilometer stretch by Light Horse units almost simultaneously. The capture of Jenin by the 3rd Light Horse Brigade coincided with the capture of Samaria and its subsequent overrunning by the 5th Australian Light Horse Brigade.[20]

Jenin was seized in the evening of 20 September while Nablus fell in the early morning darkness of the 21st. Both events coincided with darkness, against enemy forces which thought themselves secure in their rear areas. The thrusts by the Light Horse units were characterized by audacity and speed. Turkish resistance was relatively light due to these circumstances. No obstacles impeded the mounted movement.

In several instances, enemy columns, some in excess of 2,000 troops, were persuaded to surrender by bluff. Mounted units of the D.M.C. which were only a fraction the Turkish columns' sizes were able to force surrenders by ruses or as a result of the shock of a cavalry charges delivered to the column.[21]

The entire offensive surpassed the expectations of the Allied commanders. What remained was largely anticlimatic: a pursuit of broken forces north into present day Syria. The war ended over a month after the beginning of the Battle of Megiddo. There were a number of cavalry actions by all regiments of the D.M.C.[22] It was fitting that one of the last major brigade sized charges occurred on the 25th of September by the 4th Australian Light Horse Brigade, the same brigade that had won Beersheba almost a year prior.

The significance of the charge at Semakh again demonstrates the complete flexibility of the Australian Light Horse units. Although the units involved in the action were armed with the sword, they still were able to quickly revert to dismounted infantry. No indications exist that any of the other cavalry units of the D.M.C. performed the same change.

Charge at Semakh

After taking a slight pause to consolidate on the 22nd and 23rd of September, Chauvel ordered the 4th Light Horse Brigade to seize the rail station at the village of Semakh. Semakh was located on the very southern shore of the Sea of

Galilee (also known as Lake Tiberias or Lake Kinneret). It was a rail point joining both the port of Haifa on the Mediterranean and Amman.

Brigadier Grant had available for the seizure of Semakh the 11th Regiment and part of the 12th. The 4th Regiment was away on detached duty. On the morning of 24 September the Brigade moved toward Semakh hoping to join elements of the 5th Light Horse Brigade which could assist in the capture of the town. The march continued through the night and the town was approached from the south on the west side of the Jordan River without linking up with the elements of the 5th Brigade.

The 11th Regiment was taken under fire prior to sunrise south of the village of Semakh. The area to the front of the village offered no cover or concealment as the area was part of the Jordan River alluvial plain. The terrain was relatively flat and featureless. The commander of the regiment was able to discern the village about 2.5 kilometers to the north and immediately ordered the regiment to deploy into line even though it was still dark.[23]

With one squadron on the west side of the main north-south rail line, and two to the east side, the 11th Regiment formed line and charged. The regiment charged across open fields at machine guns, artillery, and infantry. The accompanying squadrons of the 12th Regiment provided suppressive fires from a flank position. A number of charging horses fell into holes in the moon light while many others were hit by machine gun fire. The regiment quickly closed on the village and over-ran the positions in front of it. They then had to dismount and begin clearing the enemy from the buildings and a number of rail cars on the siding.[24]

The final count showed that the Light Horse brigade outnumbered the enemy defenders only about two to one, much less than what is normally considered necessary for a successful attack against a prepared defense. The attacking regiment that actually closed on Semakh killed approximately one hundred and captured over three times as many. Their ratio for assaulting elements to defenders was closer to one to one.

Semakh proved again the value of mounted troops being armed with the rifle and bayonet. Unable to make use of their swords for the close in dismounted fighting, the 11th Light Horse had to resort to the rifle and bayonet to rout out the German and Turkish troops during dismounted action.

Ironically the one regiment of the 4th Light Horse Brigade which did not participate in the charge at Beersheba was still able to conduct a successful charge of its own. The 11th Regiment did not rely on the sword, but on the rifle and bayonet. The 11th Regiment fought as Light Horse had been trained to fight, by riding to the enemy positions and dismounting. Under the circumstances they would have preferred to finish the fight mounted with swords, however, the village broke up the charge and provided sufficient cover for the defenders. The Light Horsemen had no choice but to dismount and fight since the sword would have been useless in the buildings and rail cars.

The capture of Semakh signaled the last large charge of the Australians against a well prepared, defending enemy.[25] After Semakh, Turco-German forces were in full retreat and had little chance to establish prepared defenses. Almost all of the charges conducted afterwards were against hastily prepared defenses or units in the open during the pursuit of the enemy moving north. The 4th Light Horse Brigade later conducted the last brigade sized charge of the war at Kaukab near Damascus but it was against a disorganized rear guard, not a prepared defensive position.

The Battle of Megiddo was the classical use of a mounted force in the offense and it is no wonder that the battle was studied for years afterwards by military leaders. The artillery softened the opposing enemy positions, the infantry opened gaps in the enemy's line, and then the cavalry poured through to disrupt the defenses in the rear by exploitation and pursuit. The conduct of the battle was exactly what the commanders on the Western Front had been hoping to achieve during the first four years of the war and eventually were only able to partially implement in July-November 1918.

The last major battle of the campaign in Palestine was characterized by the use of the cavalry in its traditional role which had been denied in Europe. The maneuver at the Battle of Megiddo grew out of two and a half years of experience for the mounted forces in the E.E.F. The development in the use of mounted forces was led by the Australians of the Light Horse regiments, which, never composing more than 40% of the total mounted force, had a substantial impact of greater proportion than their numbers on the mounted operations of the E.E.F.

Commanded by an Australian, General Chauvel, the ANZAC Mounted Division and later the Desert Mounted Corps led the advance of the entire E.E.F. from the Suez Canal to northern Palestine and from the Jordan north to Aleppo. Its success changed the method of operations for all mounted units in the E.E.F.

Chauvel's ability as a commander throughout the entire campaign was marked by his flexibility in commanding mounted infantry and cavalry units, changing his employment in the final phase of the campaign to meet the new requirements of the situation. While it might be argued that any good corps commander should have been able to do just this, no other Western corps commander was ever required to change the use of over half his unit from a primarily infantry role to that of cavalry. The apparent ease by which this transition occurred not only speaks highly of Chauvel, but of the Light Horsemen as well.

Mobility was returned to the battlefield both tactically through the charge and operationally through the major operations of the mounted corps. The influence of Megiddo were too late in the war to affect other operations. However, the lessons of Megiddo were not forgotten and were a greater influence on cavalry operations years after the war. Megiddo became the example most commonly cited as the epitome of modern cavalry actions.

NOTES

1. Brigadier General James Parker, The Mounted Rifleman (Wisconsin: George Bants Publishing Co., 1916), p. 11.

2. Falls, Military Operations Egypt and Palestine From June 1917 to the End of the War, Part II, pp. 416-417.

3. Falls, Armageddon: 1918, p. 16.

4. Lawford, Cavalry, P. 173.

5. Emmanuel Dehan, Megiddo: Armegeddon (Tel Aviv, Israel: Published by Emmanuel Dehan, 1980), p. 8; Allenby, The Advance of the Egyptian Expeditionary Force, p. 171, plate 41.

6. McEntee, Military History of the World War, p. 55S.

7. Falls, Military Operations Egypt and Palestine From June 1917 to the End of the War, Part I, p. iii (Appendix).

8. Falls, Military Operations Egypt and Palestine From June 1917 to the End of the War, Part II, p. 413.

9. McEntee, Military History of the World War, p. 448.

10. Falls, Armageddon: 1918, p. 127.

11. Falls, Military Operations Egypt and Palestine From June 1917 to the End of the War, Part II, pp. 416-417; Horner, The Commanders, p. 79; Falls, Armageddon: 1918, p. 16.

12. McEntee, Military History of the World War, p. 559; Jones, The Australian Light Horse, pp. 145-147.

13. Starr, Forward, p. 141. The deception plan used by Allenby included the fabrication of 15,000 dummy horses and demonstrations by units assigned to the Jordan Valley. Falls, Armageddon: 1918, P. 16.

14. Jones, The Australian Light Horse, P. 135.

15. General Sir Archibald Wavell, Allenby, a Study in Greatness (New York: Oxford University Press, 1941), PP. 79-80.

16. Preston, The Desert Mounted Corps (London:

Constable and Co., Ltd., 1921), p. 16.

17. Jones, The Australian Light Horse, p. 150.

18. Allenby, The Advance of the Egyptian Expeditionary Force, plate 41.

19. Ibid., plate 42.

20. Gullett, The Australian Imperial Force in Sinai and Palestine, 1914-1918, p. 706.

21. Ibid., pp 707-708.

22. See Appendix A. Thirty five charges (or more) occurred during the campaign of the E.E.F. Only one actual charge occurred before the Australian charge at Beersheba and it was against native tribesmen, not regular soldiers. The remainder of the actions can be classified as mounted attacks, not charges. Ail charges following the Beersheba charge did so within a period of one year.

23. Firkins, The Australians in Nine Wars, p. 152; Preston, The Desert Mounted Corps, p. 249.

24. Falls, Armageddon: 1918, P. 88.

25. W. T. Massey, Allenby's Final Triumph (New York: E, P. Dutton and Co., 1920), p. 232

CHAPTER 5 - CONCLUSION

> This was an unfortunate doctrine to hand down to soldiers who might later have to compete with self confident troops who carried the lessons of tank warfare to their logical conclusions.[1]

The mounted forces of the E.E.F. literally finished the war in the Eastern Theater by themselves. The largest cavalry force in modern history was commanded by an Australian whose fellow countrymen indirectly made significant contributions not only to the campaign but to war in general.

The effects of this last cavalry battle at Megiddo left a lasting legacy among those who participated and those who studied it at military schools for years after the war. The magnitude of the success and euphoria of the victory it brought imparted a number of incorrect lessons to many who studied it later.

Technically, the results of the Middle East campaign were indirectly responsible for the retention of the horse mounted forces in a number of Western armies after the war. Additionally, the results were indirectly responsible for the retention of weapons that were associated with horse mounted forces: the sword, saber, and lance.

What is not commonly known are the contributions the Australians made to the conduct of war. One of these contributions was the temporary restoration of tactical mobility as a technique to the battlefield. However, they were not responsible for the propagation of the incorrect lessons, although they may have fallen victim to the same lessons. Such lessons include the dependence upon the horse for continued tactical mobility on the modern battlefield using a very specific and limited experience in the Middle East. What is significant about their participation in the Middle East is their particular approach to war.

The Australian approach to war was a result of their particular geographic and cultural conditions. At the turn of the century the Australians were imbued with values now attributed to the typical Australian. The effects of the Australian pastoralist on their society were important in developing pioneering traits. Even those Australians who were not from the outback enshrined these values so that it became an accepted ideal of all Australians.

The pioneering values imparted to the Australians were a direct result of the harsh land which they had developed during the previous century. Their struggle as convicts to develop the land under the control of autocratic British civilian and military rule caused the original Australians to form a unique social background. A combination of their convict ancestry and the influences of the new egalitarian society caused the Australians to develop quite differently from their British ancestors.

The Australians may have shared a common cultural background with that of the British but it was different due to the specific classes of people who immigrated from Britain. These people brought a specific set of values which were common to their class and developed further under the conditions in Australia. The result was a "collectivist" tendency in which the rights of the individual and group were strongly encouraged against the rule of the privileged and the bureaucracy.

While a large number of the Australians were not from the outback, they all shared an affiliation with their Walers. Perhaps it was a sign of the times, but the horse was important to the Australians who used them as livelihood in the outback and for transportation. The familiarity of the Australians with their horses became an attribute during the conflicts in which they participated both in South Africa and in the Middle East. This familiarization with horses reflected a general set of rural values that Australians developed as part of their cultural traits.

Under these conditions, the Australians were able to develop the characteristics which became their best known traits, initiative and flexibility. It is only natural that the Australian military of the period absorbed these specific characteristics in its citizen soldiery.

The formation of the Australian military reflected the general traits of the society. It began as a representative formation of the Australian society as a whole. Largely militia or volunteer, the military at the turn of the century reflected those values commonly associated with the Australian citizen soldiers. The Australians' views of military attributes such as discipline were necessarily different because of this. These differing views led to the development of particular methods of tactical organizations and employment.

While they shared common doctrine and organizations but their methods for implementing the doctrine were quite dissimilar. The development of mounted forces is an example. The inability of the British to exhibit the same degree of change as the Australians demonstrated in South Africa naturally led to friction between the two.

The joint conduct of the Boer War with the British Army gave the Australians a jaundiced look at the British method of operations. What came out of the Boer War was a heightened appreciation for the Australians' skills by the British and the Australians themselves. Significant to the Australians was the experience gained by its army which fought entirely as mounted infantry in South Africa. This experience provided a powerful basis for the approach to the military and the preparations for the next war.

The Boer War served to justify the Australian tactical methods and made the Australians wary of the British who failed to adapt quickly enough. The Australians gained an insight into the differences between their methods and those of the British. Some differences were deeply rooted in cultural development such as their respective views of discipline. While discipline in the British Army was manifested in a number of forms to include saluting and dress, the Australian rejected these formalities and considered traits such as loyalty to their 'mates' and deeds as the true demonstrations of discipline. This difference was not always understood by their British cousins with whom they worked in the Middle East and Europe and was a source of friction between them.

The conduct of the war in the Middle East quite clearly demonstrates examples of how the Australian traits were practiced successfully. The campaign in Egypt and Palestine forms an interesting example since both the British and Australian mounted forces fought against the same enemy there. Both faced very similar conditions such as the terrain, weather, and the general situation. The British demonstrated that they could not exercise the same initiative and flexibility as the Australians when all other factors were alike. On the contrary, while it was not the intent of this study to prove such, the British clearly demonstrated inflexibility.

It is interesting to note that in WWI both the British and Australian mounted units in the Middle East fought the same enemy under the same circumstances. What makes this comparison valid are the common factors of terrain, situation, and enemy. While these factors were key, they were not the cause of the successes for the Australians. For example, the terrain contributed to the tactical success of the Australians but it could have done as well for the British. It happens that the Australians were able to take advantage of the situation.

The terrain provided an environment which allowed the Australians to exercise their traits. However, the terrain was only a contributing factor, not the cause, for the initiative and flexibility demonstrated by the Australians. The desert environment only provided a conducive setting for the Australians to practice those attributes that they already possessed.

Analysis shows that the British failed to perform in the same manner as the Australians. The Australians clearly set the precedent in actions, not in a single case, but over an extended period of time and in a number of actions.

At the Battle of Romani, Chauvel demonstrated a high

degree of initiative which was not complemented by a participating British commander. Chauvel strove to take advantage of a unique situation during the battle by replacing his troops with those of British infantry. The Australian's understanding of the intent of the overall plan facilitated his actions without specific guidance from the commander, Lawrence. The Australian commander demonstrated flexibility by using his mounted troops to extend his flank. Both traits are clearly present in Chauvel's handling of his brigades during the fight.

Again at Beersheba, the Australian commander of the 4th Light Horse Brigade exhibited the distinct characteristics of initiative and flexibility. When placed in very similar circumstances, it was the Australian, Grant, not the British commander, that stepped forward and offered a solution to the difficult problem. Grant's ability to adapt to the situation caused the conduct of a decisive cavalry charge by mounted infantry which had major lasting effects on the remainder of the war in the Middle East.

The last major battle of the campaign at Megiddo is an excellent example of how the Australians not only affected the tactics of the campaign, but the operational employment of mounted forces as well. It was the Australian commander of the mounted forces, Chauvel, that launched his corps into the operational depth of the enemy's defenses. It was the Desert Mounted Corps that was able to exploit the destruction of the Turkish armies in a major operation which culminated in the capture of Damascus and the pursuit of the Turkish forces to the Taurus Mountains.

During an engagement in the Megiddo battle at the village of Semakh, the Australians demonstrated their tactical flexibility by quickly reverting to their mounted infantry role. This happened even though they had been armed with the sword and legitimately reclassified as 'cavalry.' They were not inhibited from adapting to the situation and fighting with rifle and bayonet when it was required. There exist no examples of the British cavalry doing the same although their doctrine provided for such actions.

The last major impact of the Australians Light Horse and the Desert Mounted Corps actions came after the end of the war. The legacy of this impact lasted into the next World War, over twenty years later. The charge by the Australians at Beersheba became the example frequently cited by cavalry historians after the war as to the applicability of horse mounted units on the modern battlefield.[2] Those who failed to consider that the horse was only a means of mobility, and that it was mobility, not the horse, that was the key to success, continued to exhort the potentials of horse units.

The entire campaign in Palestine from the battle at Beersheba until the end of the war became the rallying cry for the retention of the horse in the armies of countries such as Britain, Australia, France, and the United States. Notwithstanding the development of the internal combustion engine, the tank, and improved motor transportation in the years following the war, the retention of the horse was a battle gamely fought by cavalrymen.

The lance, once discarded except for ceremonial use in the British cavalry, was retained as a weapon until 1928. In the United States Army, the cavalry retained the sword until 1934. The British finally discarded the sword officially in 1936, however, soldiers of the Yeomanry stationed in the Middle East still carried the sword as late as 1941. The French kept their sabers and Vichy cadets at St. Cyr were still taught drill with them as late as 1942. As for the Australians, they kept their horses and swords until the outbreak of World War II when many of the Light Horse regiments were reorganized into other branches.

It may not be possible to determine if the campaign in Palestine and the Australians' influence directly affected the retention of the horse and the weapons associated with the cavalry so long in Western armies since a variety of factors affected each army differently. Factors such as military budget, development of mechanization, and the cavalry lobby among the leadership were factors each military had to contend with. The indirect affect is indisputable based upon professional writings, lectures, and texts of the post-war period.

As only one example, the texts used by cavalry schools such as the U.S. Cavalry School at Fort Riley, Kansas, emphatically cited the applicability of the horse and charge to modern warfare. In 1922, then Major George S. Patton, a leader whose name would be synonymous with armored warfare in another twenty five years, strongly advocated the retention of the horse and the use of the sword in mounted combat. His article about the Australian's charge at Beersheba in the Cavalry Journal left no doubt as to his feelings that horse cavalry was necessary.[3] Perhaps Patton was indicative of leaders at the time who incorrectly analyzed the situations and deduced from them the wrong lessons.

Patton fell into the same trap of substituting the means of the mobility, the horse, for the ends. The study of the Australian actions were beneficial for these cavalrymen even if the assessment and analysis of such actions were faulty.

The campaign in Egypt and Palestine during WWI did much to bring the Australians to the forefront as outstanding soldiers for their abilities. They did not have a monopoly on heroism or courage, for many of their British counterparts, as well as their enemies, proved to be just as valorous. However, the Australians did have a number of attributes which made them successful and decisively demonstrated that their traits affected their approach to war in both flexibility and initiative.

NOTES

1. Ellis, Cavalry, P. 177.

2. As an example of period writings, comments, and lectures, the following sources provide the general feeling of cavalrymen from the armies of the U.S., Great Britain, France, and Australia during the post-war WWI period. They all strongly advocated the use of horse mounted forces for future military applications: U.S. - The Palestine Campaigns (Cavalry School text used by officers in the troop officers courses), p. 276:

> Although it is not suggested that the peculiar circumstances which made the use of a large mass of cavalry the decisive feature of this campaign are likely to be exactly reproduced in the future, nevertheless it is thought that the conditions under which any campaign is probable during the next decade will approximate much more closely to those in Palestine than to those in France, and until we can produce machines that can go where ever cavalry can go, and that can achieve everything that cavalry can achieve, we must depend on the man and the horse to obtain really decisive results.;

Great Britain - Comments by Generals Lord Horne and General

Sir Alexander Godley both expressed concern that mechanization could not replace the horse. Winton, Harold R. To Change an Army (Lawrence, KS: University Press of Kansas, 1988), p. 29. Winton also gives a good description of both Godley's and General Sir R. G. Eggerton's views for retaining horse cavalry in 1926. While these officers might have been a minority, they were powerful men as was Allenby.; France - Lectures given to the French Staff College by Lieutenant-Colonel Prioux cited the importance of the horse on the modern battlefield in a lecture to the French Army War College entitled "Course in Cavalry" (1923-1924); Australia - General Chauvel's comments to Australian Army officers after the war reflected his firm conviction that there was still a place on the modern battlefield for the horse. As the Inspector-General, Commonwealth of Australia, Department of Defence, he stated in 1920 that "...the horse-soldier is just as valuable in modern warfare as he has been in the past." (Preston, The Desert Mounted Corps, p. vii). All these countries maintained large mounted formations of at least divisional size until World War II. The U.S. Army had two horse mounted cavalry divisions during the early war of which one was converted to infantry.

    3. Major George S. Patton, "What the World War Did for Cavalry." Armor (formerly the Cavalry Journal) (May -

June 1985): 8-11. Patton described the battle at the end of his article, however, he made a major factual error. He cites the sword as the cause of the majority of deaths of the Turkish defenders. This is obviously incorrect since the Light Horse brigade was not issued swords for another nine months. Patton's vested interest in the design and use of the Model 1913 U.S. Cavalry sword (commonly called the "Patton saber" since he had a major influence in its design) might explain his "mistake."

EQUIPMENT LIST, LIGHT HORSE TROOPER 1917-1918

Rider's Equipment

1 Slouch hat with chin strap and pugaree

1 Set Emu plumes

1 Large rising sun, hat badge, black

1 Service dress jacket, khaki/brown, wool

2 Small rising suns, collar dogs, black

2 Australia badges, black

1 Shirt

1 Pair breeches, bedford cord

1 Pair braces

1 Pair brown leggings

1 Pair brown lace up boots

1 Pair regulation spurs with butterflies

1 Brown leather waist belt 1 3/4" wide

1 SMLE .303 Rifle MK 111 or MK 111* and sling

1 1907 pattern bayonet to fit MK 111 or MK 111*

1 1907 pattern bayonet scabbard

1 Brown leather bayonet frog to suit above bayonet

1 1908 Pattern brown 9 pocket bandolier

Horse Equipment

1 1902 pattern bridle and headstall

1 White rope lanyard, neck rope

1 1903 or 1912 pattern saddle

1 Girth, 4 buckle

Surcingle

1 Brown woolen saddle blanket 6' X 5'

1 Set saddle wallets

1 Set double buckle straps, to secure wallet/great coat to saddle

1 Shoe case

Extra Items to be Carried for Full Marching Order

1 Mess tin

1 Canvas mess tin cover, khaki

1 Feed bag, khaki

1 Bivvy sheet khaki rolled with grey blanket

1 Great coat

1 9 Pocket brown bandolier

1 7/8 X 20" strap, centre, rear

1 7/8 X 24" strap, centre, front

1 Universal strap, shoe case to girth

4 3/4 X 20" strap, bivvy sheet

2 3/4 X 24" strap, great coat

1 3/4 X 28" strap, mess tin, shoe case to saddle

1 Ground sheet, khaki, rubberized

Extra Items to be Carried for Full Marching Order

1 1908 Pattern Khaki canvas haversack and leather strap

1 Water bottle and carrier

2 10 rd belt pouches

2 15 rd belt pouches

NOTE: This list was provided by Mr. John Hutton, Queensland Mounted Infantry Historical Troop, Light Horse Association.

SELECTED BIBLIOGRAPHY

PRIMARY SOURCES

Books

Allenby, General Sir Edmund H. H. <u>The Advance of the Egyptian Expeditionary Force.</u> London: His Majesty's Stationery Office, 1919.

Carley, T. H., MAJ, O.B.E. <u>With the Ninth Light Horse in the Great War.</u> Adelaide: The Hassell Press, 1924.

Gullett, H. S. <u>The Australian Imperial Force in Sinai and Palestine, 1914-1918.</u> Sydney: Angus and Robertson, Ltd., 1923.

Idriess, Ion L. <u>The Desert Column.</u> Sydney: Halstead Printing Co., Ltd., 1932.

Lewis, Brian B. <u>Our War: Australia</u> During World War I. Melbourne: Hogbin, Poole (Printers) Pty Ltd, 1980.

Lock, H. 0., Major. <u>With the British Army in the Holy Land.</u> London: Robert Scott Roxburghe House, 1919.

MacMunn, George, Lieutenant-General Sir, and Falls, Cyril, Captain. Official History of the War - Egypt and Palestine. London: His Majesty's Stationery Office, :1928.

Murray, Sir Archibald. Sir Archibald Murray's Despatches. London: J. M. Dent and Sons, Ltd., 1920.

Patterson, Banjo. Happy Dispatches. Sydney: Lansdowne Press, 1980.

Preston, R. M. P., Lieutenant-Colonel. The Desert Mounted Corps. London: Constable and Co., Ltd., 1921.

Richardson, J. D., Lieutenant-Colonel, DSO. 7th Light Horse Regiment A.I.F. Sydney: Radcliffe Press, 1923.

von Sanders, Liman, General of Cavalry. Five Years In Turkey. Annapolis: The U.S. Naval Institute, 1927.

Teichman, 0., Captain. The Diary of a Yeomanry M.O. London: T. Fisher Unwin Ltd., 1921.

Wavell, A. P Lieutenant-General. The Palestine Campaigns. London: Constable and Co., Ltd., 1928.

Australian Government Documents

Light Horse Manual: Drill Training and Exercise of the Light Horse Regiment. Melbourne: J. Hemp, Government Printer, 1 January 1910.

The Australian Army: A Brief History. Canberra: Australian Government Publishing Service, 1983.

British Government Documents

Field Service Manual, Mounted Infantry. London: War Office, 1899.

Regulations for Mounted Infantry. London: Her Majesty's Stationery Office, 1884.

Yeomanry and Mounted Rifle Training, Parts I and II, 1912. Warrington and London: Mackie and Co., Ltd., 1912.

United States Government Documents

Cavalry Operations During World War. Fort Riley, KS: The Cavalry School, 1929.

FM 100-5, Operations. Headquarters, Department of the Army, 5 May 1986.

History of the Cavalry During the World War, Vol II. Fort Riley, KS: U.S. Cavalry School, 1924.

Unpublished Materials

Prioux, Lieutenant-Colonel. Translated by Captain W. B. Bradford. "Course in Cavalry." Lecture presented to the French Army War College, Ecole Superieure de Guerre, 1923-1924.

Walker, Kirby, Colonel. "The Palestine Campaign, Part I." Fort Riley, KS: The Cavalry School, 1921.

"The Palestine Campaign." Fort Riley, KS: The Cavalry School, 1922-1923.

Other Sources

ANZACS. Produced by Geoff Burrowes and directed by George Miller. 165 min. Celebrity Home Entertainment, 1986.

Videocassette.

Forty Thousand Horsemen. Produced and directed by Charles Chauvel. 84 min. Yesteryear Productions, 1941. Videocassette.

Gallipoli. Produced by Robert Stigwood and Patricia Lovel. 110 min. 1981. Videocassette.

The Light Horsemen. Produced by Simon Wincer and directed by Ian Jones and Simon Wincer. RKO Pictures, 106 min. 1988. Videocassette.

The Man From Snowy River. Produced by Geoff Burrowes-Miller and directed by Keith Wagstaff. 104 min. 20th Century Fox, 1982. Videocassette.

Soldiers: A History of Men in Battle (Cavalry). Produced by Robert Toner. 55 min. BBC, 1985. Videocassette.

SECONDARY SOURCES

Adam-Smith, Patsy. The ANZACS. West Melbourne: Thomas Nelson Australia Pty. Ltd., 1978.

Barthorp, Michael. British Cavalry Uniforms Since 1660. Poole, U.K.: Blandford Press, 1984.

Barthorp, Michael. The Anglo-Boer Wars. Poole, U.K.: Blandford Press, 1987.

Bates, I.B., Major. Queensland Mounted Units, 1860-1940. Brisbane, Australia: Victoria Barracks Museum and Historical Society, 1988.

Brereton, J. M. The Horse In War. New York: Arco Publishing Co., Inc., 1976.

Bullock, David L. Allenby's War: The Palestine-Arabian Campaigns 1916-1918. London: Blandford Press, 1988.

Chappell, Mike. British Cavalry Equipments, 1800-1941. London: Osprey Publishing Ltd., 1983.

Chappell, Mike. British Infantry Equipments, 1908-80. London: Osprey Publishing Ltd., 1980.

Cohen, Eliot, and Gooch, John. Military Misfortunes: The

Anatomy of Failure in War. New York: The Free Press, 1990.

Cocker, Mark. Richard Meinertzhagen: Soldier, Scientist and Spy. London: Secker and Warburg, 1989.

Dane, Edmund. British Campaigns in the Near East, 1914 - 1918, Vol. 2. London: Hodder and Stoughton, 1919.

Davey, Arthur, ed. Breaker Morant and the Bushveldt Carbineers. Capetown, South Africa: Van Riebeeck Society, 1987.

Dehan, Emmanuel. Megiddo: Armegeddon. Tel Aviv, Israel: Published by Emmanuel Dehan, 1980.

Dennison, George T., Lieutenant Colonel. History of the Cavalry from the Earliest Times, With Lessons for the Future. London: MacMillan and Co., 1877.

Ellis, John. Cavalry. New York: G. P. Putnam's Sons, 1978.
Falls, Cyril, Captain. Military Operations Eygpt and Palestine From June 1917 to the End of the War, Part I. London: His Majesty's Stationery Office, 1930.

Falls, Cyril, Captain. <u>Military Operations Eygpt and Palestine From June 1917 to the End of the War, Part II,</u> London: His Majesty's Stationery Office, 1930.

Falls, Cyril, Captain and Major A. F. Becke. <u>Military Operations in Egypt and Palestine From June 1917 to the End of the War, Maps,</u> London: His Majesty's Stationery Office, 1930.

Falls, Cyril. <u>Armageddon: 1918.</u> The Nautical and Aviation Publishing Company of America, 1964.

Firkins, Peter. <u>The Australians In Nine Wars.</u> New York: McGraw-Hill Book Company, 1971.

Fraser, W. B. <u>Always A Strathcona.</u> Calgary, Canada: Comprint Publishing Co., 1976.

Galloway, William Johnson, M.P., <u>Advanced Australia: A Short Account of Australia on the Eve of Federation.</u> London: Methuen and Co., 1899.

Greenhous, Brereton. <u>Dragoon: The Centennial History of the Royal Canadian Dragoons, 1883-1983.</u> Ottawa, Canada:

Campbell Corporation, 1983.

Greenwood, Gordon, ed. Australia, A Social and Political History, New York: Frederick A. Praeger, 1955.

Griess, Thomas, ed. Atlas for the Great War. Wayne, N.J.: Avery Publishing, 1986.

Herr, John K. and, Wallace, Edward S. The Story of the U.S. Cavalry, 1775-1942. Boston: Little, Brown, 1953.

Hill, A. J. Chauvel of the Light Horse. Victoria (Australia): Melbourne University Press, 1978.

Horner, D. M., ed. The Commanders. Sydney: George, Allen and Unwin, 1984.

Hughes, Robert. The Fatal Shore. New York: Vintage Books, 1986.

Jones, Ian. The Australian Light Horse. Sydney: Time-Life Books, 1987.

Laffin, John. The Australian Army at War, 1899-1975. London:

Osprey Publishing, 1982.

Laffin, John. ANZACS at War. London: Abelard-Shuman Ltd., 1965.

Laird, John. The Australian Experience of War. Melbourne: Mead and Beckett Publishing, 1988.

Larson, Robert H. The British Army and the Theory of Armored Warfare, 1918-1940. Newark: University of Delaware Presses, 1984.

Lawford, James, ed. Techniques and Triumphs of the Military Horseman: The Stories of the Great Cavalry Regiments, Their Commanders and Celebrated Actions - Cavalry. Indianapolis: Bobbs-Merrill, 1976.

Livsey, Anthony. Great Battles of WWI. New York: MacMillan Publishing Co., 1989.

Lunt, James D. Charge to Glory. New York: Harcourt Brace and Co., 1960.

McEntee, Lindsley. Military History of the World War. New

York: Charles Scribner's Sons, 1943.

McLeod, A.L., ed. The Pattern of Australian Culture. Ithaca, N.Y.: Cornell University Press, 1963.

MacMunn, George, Lieutenant-General Sir. Military Operations Eyqpt and Palestine. Maps; no other information on carton.

Massey, W. T. Allenby's Final Triumph. New York: E. P. Dutton and Company, 1920.

Massey, W. T. How Jerusalem Was Won. New York: Charles Schribner's Sons, 1920.

Mendham, Dawn. The ANZAC Tradition. Canberra: Canberra Press, 1990.

Messenger, Charles. History of the British Army. Novato, CA: Presidio Press, 1986.

Pakenham, Thomas. The Boer War. New York: Random House, 1979.

Paret, Peter, ed. Makers of Modern Strategy from Machiavelli to the Nuclear Age. Princeton, N.J.: Princeton University Press, 1986.

Parker, James, Brigadier General. The Mounted Rifleman. Menasha, Wisconsin: George Banta Publishing Co., 1916.

Robson, L. L. The First A.I.F.: A Study of it Recruitment 1914-1918, Hong Kong: Silex Enterprise and Printing Co., 1970.

Sawicki, James A. Cavalry Regiments of the US Army. Dumfries, VA: Wyvern Publications, 1985.

Schmitt, Bernadotte, and Vedeler, Harold C. The Rise of Modern Europe: The World in the Crucible 1914-1919. New York: Harper and Row, Publishers, 1984.

Smith, W. H. B. Small Arms of the World. New York City: Gallahad Books, 1973.

Starr, Joan and, Sweeney, Christopher. Forward: The History of the 2/14th Light Horse (Queensland Mounted Infantry),

Queensland, Australia: University of Queensland Press, 1989.

Taylor, Griffith. Australia. Sydney: E. P. Dutton and Co., Inc., 1943.

Truscott, Lucian K., Jr., General. The Twilight of the U.S. Cavalry. Lawrence, Kansas: University Press of Kansas, 1989.

Turner, Joseph William. The Last Bright Blades: A Study of the Cavalry Saber from 1904 to 1934. Atascadero, CA: The Wagapaw Press, 1982.

Tylden, Major G. Horses and Saddlery. London: J. A. Allen and Company, 1965.

Wallace, R. L. The Australians at the Boer War. Canberra: The Australian War Memorial and the Australian Government Publishing Service, 1976.

Ward, Russel. The Australian Legend. Melbourne: Oxford University Press, 1958.

Warner, Philip. The British Cavalry. Melbourne: J. M. Dent and Sons Ltd., 1984.

Wavell, Archibald, General Sir. Allenby, A Study in Greatness.

New York: Oxford University Press, 1941.

Winton, Harold R. To Change An Army. Lawrence, Kansas: University Press of Kansas, 1988.

The Cavalry School, ed. Cavalry Combat. Harrisburg, PA: The Telegraph Press, 1937.

Periodicals and Articles

Cummings, Mike. "Harking Back, The Australian Light Horse." Hoofs and Horns. November 1984, pp. 44-45.

Gudmundsson, Bruce I. "A Lesson from the Boers." Military History Quarterly, Vol. 1, No. 4 (Summer 1989): 34-35.

Macalpine, Ross. "Australian Military Saddles." Horse Mounted Detachment, Parramatta Barracks, Parramatta, Australia, 1987.

Morris, Roy, Jr. "Surfeit of Commanders." Military History. June 1990, pp. 38-45.

Patton, George S., Major. "What the World War Did for

Cavalry." Armor (originally printed in the former The Cavalry Journal, 1922) (May-June 1985): 8-11.

Weir, William. "Advantage Sought On High Ground." Military History, August 1986, pp. 34-40.

"The Wonderful Waler, Warhorse Supreme." Australian Horse and Rider, November 1975, pp. 8-11.

Printed in Great Britain
by Amazon